How to Read Egyptian Hieroglyphs

How to Read

Egyptian Hieroglyphs

A STEP-BY-STEP GUIDE TO TEACH YOURSELF

Mark Collier and Bill Manley

New illustrations by Richard Parkinson

University of California Press

Berkeley   Los Angeles   London

University of California Press
Berkeley and Los Angeles, California

University of California Press, Ltd.
London, England

Published by arrangement with the
British Museum Press

ISBN 0-520-21597-4

Designed by Andrew Shoolbred
Typeset in Meridien by Nigel Strudwick, using
hieroglyphs from the Cleo Font designed by Cleo
Huggins. Extra diacritics and hieroglyphs by
Nigel Strudwick.

Cover design: Kenneth Carroll
Cover: Inscription on a ritual implement,
dedicated by King Senwosret I to his ancestor
King Mentjuhotep II. For an explanation of the
inscription, see page 126. The Metropolitan
Museum of Art, New York, acc. no. 24.21, Rogers
Fund, 1924.

Printed in Great Britain

9   8   7   6   5   4

Contents

Introduction

The aim of this book is to enable you to read and enjoy the hieroglyphs and the language of ancient Egypt. It is chiefly aimed at those who have had no previous experience of reading hieroglyphs, but should also benefit others who would like to improve their knowledge in line with contemporary research. Above all, this is a practical guide: from the very beginning you will be introduced to genuine hieroglyphic texts, with full supporting explanations and study aids. In order to do this, we have concentrated on monuments in the British Museum, in particular the stelae (or funerary inscriptions) of Egyptian officials, as well as coffins, tomb scenes, and the famous Abydos King-list of Ramesses II. Each chapter introduces you to a new feature of the hieroglyphic script or the language, and ends with copies of inscriptions on which you can practise your skills. We believe this approach has a number of advantages.

First, by reading genuine ancient inscriptions from the first lesson, you can build up your familiarity with the tricks of the trade: everything here (from individual signs to whole inscriptions) is typical of the kind of monuments displayed, not just in the British Museum, but in museums throughout the world. Secondly, by reading these monuments, we hope you will feel a real sense of achievement at each stage of the book. Thirdly, concentrating on a coherent group of monuments will allow us to raise some important topics – such as the role of Osiris, god of the dead, and the Mysteries celebrated at his cult centre, Abydos – which will help you to understand the cultural background of these monuments.

Rather than cramming in unnecessary detail, we will give you plenty of practice in reading hieroglyphs, and introduce you to the most common features of the ancient Egyptian language as it appears on these monuments. This will give you a firm basis on which to build, if you later move on to study other genres of the wealth of texts which survives from ancient Egypt – literature, religious wisdom, royal decrees, or whatever.

This book has developed out of a course which we have been teaching since 1992. It was clear to us back then that the existing introductions to ancient Egyptian were either too brief or too detailed, and that there was a need for an up-to-date course adapted to the needs of beginners studying at home. We have taught the course in various guises for several groups and institutions: the University of London Centre for Extra-Mural Studies, the Egypt Exploration Society, the University of Glasgow, the Workers Educational Association, the Sussex Egyptology Society and the Thames Valley Egyptological Society at the University of Reading. At the Bloomsbury Summer School in particular, we have had the chance to introduce people to hieroglyphs in the hot-house of a single, concentrated week of study. This book owes a great deal to the constructive feedback of the students at all these venues, who have helped us (sometimes forced us!) to refine and clarify the text, and as a result it is much clearer and more accessible. Although it would be impossible to acknowledge so many by name, we are immensely grateful to each and every one of them for their enthusiasm and feedback, and for encouraging us in our belief that this book – and the approach it embodies – is a worthwhile project.

In developing this project into book form, we have had the good fortune to be able to draw on the knowledge and support of many people. At the British Museum, Vivian Davies, Keeper of Egyptian Antiquities, first brought the project to the attention of British Museum Press, and encouraged us to make use of Richard Parkinson's expertise in copying hieroglyphic monuments; Stephen Quirke freely shared his considerable knowledge of Middle Kingdom officialdom, as well as encouragement and the first round of drinks; as noted, we are especially grateful to Richard Parkinson for his outstanding line drawings. At Bloomsbury Summer School, we would like to thank the Director, Christopher Coleman, who allowed us carte blanche to develop language courses, and also his admirable staff for diligently keeping us all (tutors and students) alive. Several colleagues have helped us to teach hieroglyphs at the School: Ludwig Morenz, Toby Wilkinson, and especially José-Ramon Pérez-Accino, who is now a regular partner in our teaching. At the University of London Centre for Extra-Mural Studies, our grateful thanks are due to Tony Legge and Lesley Hannigan, who allowed us the freedom to develop the course as we saw fit, and also to Louise Lambe. Mark drafted his contributions to the book while a resident Fellow at All Souls College, Oxford, and completed them after his appointment to the School of Archaeology, Classics and Oriental Studies, University of Liverpool; he would like to acknowledge the support of both these institutions. His work on the language sections of the book has developed in tandem with his comprehensive undergraduate grammar course, *Introduction to Middle Egyptian*, which will be published separately.

We are grateful to the staff of the British Museum Press, not least for agreeing to take on such a complex book; above all our editor, Carolyn Jones, for her dedication and good humour in dealing with such a demanding project. We would specially like to thank Nigel Strudwick for undertaking the English and Egyptian typesetting, and Helen Strudwick for correcting proofs in Nigel's absence. Finally our thanks are due to Mark Mechan, who prepared the map of Abydos on page 55.

It is customary to add a final word about partners, but in the present case our love and genuine heartfelt thanks are due to our wives, Joanne Timpson and Kathy McFall, who have put up with us, and this project, for a long time. In particular, Joanne, as well as coping with the arrival of Oliver and a preoccupied husband, still found time to comment on the final draft.

Mark Collier
Bill Manley

Illustrations

The line drawings of the stelae reproduced in this book were drawn by Richard Parkinson, Department of Egyptian Antiquities, British Museum. The scenes from the Middle Kingdom tombs at Meir are from A.M. Blackman, *The Rock Tombs of Meir*, vols I and II, Egypt Exploration Society, London 1914 and 1915; we are grateful to the Society for permission to reproduce them. The photographs on pages 31, 44, 63, 64, 108 and 125 are supplied courtesy of the Trustees of the British Museum, © British Museum Photographic Service. Mark Mechan prepared the map of Abydos on page 55.

Authors' note: Due to refurbishment work at the British Museum during 1997-8, it has not always been possible for the authors to collate their own copies against the original monuments.

Chapter 1

Hieroglyphs

§1 Introduction

Hieroglyphs are pictures used as signs in writing. Many depict living creatures or objects (or their parts):

owl   seated man   mouth   water-pot

And, as you might expect, some signs represent the object they depict. So, for example, the mouth-sign ⬯ is used to write the word for mouth, usually in combination with a stroke-sign (see §13 below for this sign):

r mouth

However, very few words are actually written in this way. Instead, hieroglyphic picture-signs are used to convey the *sound* (and meaning) of the ancient Egyptian language, just as the letters of our own alphabet convey the sounds of English. So, for example, the hieroglyphs above the figure roasting the goose do not read 'reed, chick, man, face' etc., which makes no sense; rather, they convey the sounds of various words in Egyptian which together have the following meaning:

'I have been roasting since the beginning of time – I have never seen the like of this goose'
(Meir III, pl. 23)

The purpose of this book is to show you just how this is done.

Reading hieroglyphs

How then can hieroglyphs be read to show us something of the sound of an ancient Egyptian word? The easiest way to see this is through looking at a real example. The sign ⌑ depicts a schematic house (in plan) and is used to write the word for 'house' as follows (I is the stroke-sign already noted above):

$$pr \quad \text{house}$$

As it happens, this word is based on the two consonants p and r combined to give pr. We shall discuss the way the ancient Egyptian word is put into our own writing system – how it is *transliterated* – in §§3 and 4 below. Now, there is another word which makes use of the same sound combination p and r, the word for 'go out', 'leave'. In hieroglyphs this is written as:

$$pr \quad \text{go out, leave}$$

In this word, ⌑ is no longer being used to depict a house, but rather to 'picture' the sound combination pr (this is discussed in Chapter 2). Put more formally, ⌑ is being used as a *sound-sign* or *phonogram*. This is termed the *rebus principle*; it is as if we were to write the English word *belief* with a picture of a bee and a leaf as 🐝🍃. On this basis hieroglyphs can be used to indicate *sounds* rather than things and can thus be used in words quite unrelated in meaning to the objects they depict.

The word ⌑ pr, 'go out', also displays another two signs whose use will be explained more fully later. The mouth-sign ⬭ reads r as it did in ⬭ r 'mouth', although it has nothing to do with 'mouth' here, being used instead to *complement* or clarify the reading of ⌑ pr (this is discussed in Chapter 2). The walking legs ⋀ are used as a *determinative*, a sign sometimes placed at the end of a word to give a general idea of its meaning, here of motion (see §6 below).

§3 Transliteration

In the last section we rendered ⌑ into our writing system as pr. It is the normal practice among Egyptologists to *transliterate* the sounds of a hieroglyphic word in this way. It is a very good discipline to get used to this right from the beginning and we encourage you always to transliterate when reading. The only real oddity about this is that hieroglyphs are not used to write vowels (a, e, i, o, u), only consonants; although this will seem a bit strange at first, you should soon get used to it.

§4 1-consonant signs

It is now time to get you started reading hieroglyphs for yourself. The most important hieroglyphs are the 1-consonant signs, where each hieroglyph contributes a single sound towards the reading of a word, rather like the letters of our own alphabet:

SIGN	TRANS-LIT.	SAY	SIGN	TRANS-LIT.	SAY	SIGN	TRANS-LIT.	SAY
𓄿	*ꜣ*	a	𓄿	*m*	m	𓈙	*š*	sh
𓇋	*i*	i/a	﹋	*n*	n	𓎡	*ḳ*	k
𓏭 or ＼＼	*y*	y	⟶	*r*	r	𓎡	*k*	k
▬	*ꜥ*	a	𓉐	*h*	h	𓎼	*g*	g
𓅱 or ℮	*w*	w/u	𓎺	*ḥ*	h	𓏏	*t*	t
𓃀	*b*	b	⊜	*ḫ*	kh	𓍿	*ṯ*	tj
𓊪	*p*	p	⟿	*ẖ*	kh	𓂧	*d*	d
𓆑	*f*	f	𓊽 or ⟿	*s*	s	𓆓	*ḏ*	j

We shall concentrate here on the reading of these signs. If you wish to identify the objects the signs depict, consult the full sign-list beginning on p. 129.

The proper value of each sign is the transliteration value given in the second column; the third column simply gives a way in which we, as English speakers, can vocalise these signs for our own convenience.

Most of these sounds resemble their English counterparts and can be transliterated directly into familiar letters from our own alphabet. However, some 1-consonant signs are used to represent sounds not present in spoken or written English, and these require specially adapted transliteration symbols of their own:

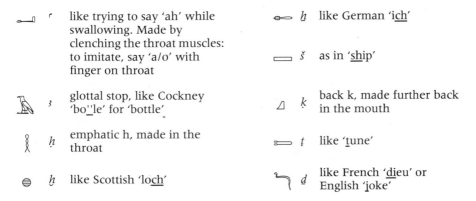

▬ *ꜥ*	like trying to say 'ah' while swallowing. Made by clenching the throat muscles: to imitate, say 'a/o' with finger on throat	⟿ *ẖ* like German 'i<u>ch</u>'
𓄿 *ꜣ*	glottal stop, like Cockney 'bo''le' for 'bottle'	▭ *š* as in '<u>sh</u>ip'
𓎺 *ḥ*	emphatic h, made in the throat	𓎡 *ḳ* back k, made further back in the mouth
⊜ *ḫ*	like Scottish 'lo<u>ch</u>'	𓍿 *ṯ* like '<u>t</u>une'
		𓆓 *ḏ* like French '<u>di</u>eu' or English '<u>j</u>oke'

Each 1-consonant sign represents a distinct sound in the ancient Egyptian language and so each needs its own transliteration symbol. It is important to include all the various dots and dashes when transliterating – they are not optional. In transliteration you should use the proper symbol given in the *second* column of the table on p. 3. This is true even if we find it difficult to tell the difference between two sounds. For example, ḳ and k are quite different sounds in Egyptian, even though distinguishing between them is rather difficult for us as English speakers.

There is no need to try and pronounce ancient Egyptian words exactly (in any case this is impossible, since the vowels are not written out for us). However, it is useful to be able to read out your transliterations and vocalise whole words, rather than spelling them out sign by sign. So, a purely conventional pronunciation, entirely for our convenience, is usually adopted. These are the renderings given in the third column in the table on p. 3. Many signs have values similar to letters of our own alphabet and present no problem, whereas the more unusual ones are usually given a convenient English approximation. We also need to add vowels. The convention normally adopted is to insert an 'e' between each consonant, except in the cases of ꜣ and ꜥ, where 'a' is used, and *w*, where 'u' is sometimes used because they are easier to pronounce. Once again, these pronunciations are purely a practical convenience and are not intended to bear any relation to spoken Egyptian. For example, the following is the word for 'birds', *ꜣpdw* (a writing discussed in §8), given with its transliteration and its English meaning:

$$\text{🦅 ▢ 🦆 }\quad \text{ꜣpdw} \quad \text{birds}$$

Purely for our own convenience we could pronounce this 'apedu'.

§5 Arrangement of signs

It may already have struck you, from looking at the examples discussed so far, that hieroglyphs are not arranged one after the other as in our own alphabetic system, but in balanced groups or 'blocks' arranged to fill the available space. In particular, some signs are placed over others in order to fill the space in a more pleasing manner. As an example, here is the name of the official Senbi (*snbi*) from Exercise 1.8 on p. 13:

The name is written from left to right, starting with the *s* (1). But notice that the signs making up the name are grouped together, so that the *n* (2), as a long thin sign, is placed above both the tall thin signs for *b* (3) and *i* (4), forming a block. The rule for such arrangements is quite simple: when you meet a block of hieroglyphs, read the top one(s) before the bottom one(s) and then carry on as normal. You will see a number of examples of grouping throughout the rest of this chapter. You may wish to read this paragraph again when reading §7 on the direction of writing.

At this point, you may wish to attempt Exercises 1.1 and 1.2 on pp. 10-11.

§6 Determinatives: meaning-signs

So far we have studied words written out with sound-signs alone. However, in hieroglyphic writing words are sometimes written with meaning-signs, or *determinatives*, placed at the end of the word after the sound-signs. The following are examples of some common determinatives and words written with them:

𓀜	man and his occupations	𓀀	*s*	man
𓀀	god, king	𓀭	*skr*	(the god) Soker
☉	sun, light, time	𓉔𓂋𓅱☉	*hrw*	day
⏴	motion	𓉔𓄿𓃀⏴	*hȝb*	send
𓅪	small bird used for bad, weak or little things	*bin*	bad, evil
⊗	town, village	𓎡𓇋⊗	*ḳis*	Qis (place-name)

Determinatives do not contribute to the sounds of the word and so are not transliterated. From our point of view, they simply help us to get some general idea of the meaning of a word. A large number of signs can be used as determinatives, but for two reasons this fact should not get in your way. First, as already mentioned, we do not transliterate determinatives, so they do not need to be at the centre of your attention, especially early on in your studies. Secondly, in the inscriptions you will be reading in this book determinatives are quite frequently omitted. However, if you are bothered by a particular determinative, consult the full sign-list beginning on p. 129.

Two other common determinatives require a little more description. 𓀁 (not to be confused with 𓀜 'man') is the meaning-sign used with words for what can be taken in or expelled through the mouth, either literally (eating, speaking) or metaphorically (emotions, attitudes, thinking) as well as the relevant activities connected with these, for example:

𓇋𓇋𓀁   *nis*   call out, summon

The most common determinative, however, is ⸗, the papyrus roll, used for abstract words or concepts. Although such words could not easily be represented by a picture, they could be written down, for example on papyrus, thus acquiring a tangible physical form. This written form could then be depicted in the shape of the rolled-up papyrus sheet:

snb   health, healthy

sḫr   counsel, plan, conduct, manner

One important word often written with the papyrus roll determinative is:

ḫt   thing(s)

The word *ḫt* is often written with the plural strokes ၊ ၊ ၊ (see §8 below), although it is not itself a plural word. Notice that, for reasons of spacing, the papyrus roll can be positioned either horizontally or vertically – you will find that a number of long thin signs can be arranged like this.

Sometimes a word can have more than one determinative:

nḏs   individual, ordinary man, person (from root meaning 'little, small')

Having a determinative thus gives us a second way of getting at a word – a general clue as to its meaning. This has the advantage that we can distinguish between two words written with the same sound-signs:

ỉꜣw   old, the old   *ỉꜣw*   adoration, praise

As we shall see in Chapter 2, there are other features of the hieroglyphic script which tend to ensure that different words are written differently even when they share the same sounds.

In practice, however, as on the monumental inscriptions we shall be studying in this book, determinatives are often omitted. For example, in Exercise 1.2 you are asked to transliterate the following words (from the roasting scene in §1) without determinatives. They are shown here alongside examples with a determinative:

or   roast   or   goose

At this point, you may wish to attempt Exercise 1.3 on p. 11.

§7 Direction of writing

So far, we have ordered the hieroglyphs following our own system of writing, i.e. writing them in lines from left to right. However, hieroglyphs were used in a more decorative manner than letters in our writing system; in particular, they often formed a fundamental part of the aesthetic scheme of a monument. Although we shall continue to present the hieroglyphs in left-to-right order within the text of this book, when you study real examples of inscriptions, these may well be organised from right to left (this is in fact the more usual direction) and possibly in columns. Fortunately, there is a very simple trick to reading hieroglyphs in the right order:

Read into the front or faces of the various signs, and from above to below.

Put another way, signs normally look towards the beginning of the text.

So, if we look at the following scene, the hieroglyphs are to be read in the order numbered. Notice that the orientation of a figure helps, particularly when there are not many signs with a clear 'front':

Offering scene from the tomb of Senbi at Meir (read from right to left) (Meir I, pl. 9)

In this case, the inscription is fitted into the space surrounding the figure. The overall direction of writing is indicated best by the foot-sign (10): to read into the front of this sign we need to read from right to left, the direction we would also need to look into the face of the accompanying figure. Vertically, we always read from top to bottom (see §5 above), so the text begins at the top right. The first three signs read horizontally above the top of the foreleg of beef carried by the figure. The remaining signs then read down the column, but still from right to left within each block, as indicated by nos 4-13. You may well recognise the name of Senbi discussed in §5 above. Compare the right-to-left writing of this name (nos 8-11) with the left-to-right ordering given in §5 (taken from another inscription in Senbi's tomb). To increase your confidence in this skill, a full vocabulary for this inscription is provided at the end of this chapter, so that you can practise reading it for yourself.

As an example reading from left to right, we can look once more at the inscription we used to introduce this book, shown on p. 8 with the order of the signs of the first line.

In this example, there are two rows of inscriptions, an upper one which is read first and a lower one, read second. Notice, once again, that the hieroglyphs have been fitted around the figure. So, Line 1 reads from left to right horizontally (reading into the face of the chick, the seated man, the owl and the bird in flight) and then at the end turns the corner, as it were, dropping down to finish in a column with nos 13-15. As with our writing system, we then return to the start of the next line and read along once more (into the face of signs such as the seated man and the chick).

As these examples also indicate, hieroglyphic signs were placed in a continuous sequence without any punctuation marks or word spacings. No doubt this will seem quite intimidating at first, but we hope to show you by example that, as you become familiar with the script and gain a grasp of useful words, this is nothing like as bad as it might seem. Exercise 1.8 (see pp. 13–14) will give you further practice in this skill.

§8 ⟨ *i* and ⟨ *w* and plurals

Hieroglyphic writing is quite economical. Along with vowels, the consonants ⟨ *i* and ⟨ *w* are often omitted in writing, except at the beginning of words. This is particularly true for grammatical endings. For example, the plural is indicated by a *-w* ending (just as it is typically indicated in English by adding '-s', as in 'bird', 'birds'); this is sometimes fully written out, but more often the *-w* is omitted. The word for 'bird' (singular) is:

⟨image⟩   *ȝpd*   bird, fowl

For our convenience this word can be sounded 'aped'.

This is made plural by adding on a *-w*. A plural determinative of three strokes ı ı ı is also usually added. Since the determinative ı ı ı suffices to indicate the plural, the -*w* ending is often simply left out of the writing (and transliterated in brackets), leaving a more compact group of hieroglyphs:

or   *ȝpdw* or *ȝpd(w)*   birds

§9 Nouns

Learning to read hieroglyphs is, however, only one part of reading a hieroglyphic inscription, especially if you aspire to making real progress with your studies. Since hieroglyphs were used by the ancient Egyptians to write down their own language, it is necessary to build up a familiarity with how words are put together in Egyptian. Throughout this book, we will introduce you step by step to the most common features of ancient Egyptian which you are likely to meet in the sort of inscriptions studied here. Some of the ways Egyptian works are rather like English, and so will seem quite normal to you, but some of its features are not as we would expect from English, and will need a little more discussion and thought.

As a starting point, it is useful to know something about nouns in Egyptian (nouns are the words typically used to refer to people, objects, living things and the like). In Egyptian, all nouns are treated as being either masculine or feminine, even if there is no obvious reason (to us) why this should be the case; you may be familiar with a similar convention in French. Fortunately, this distinction is very easy to spot in ancient Egyptian, since feminine nouns almost always end in ⌒ -*t*, whereas masculine nouns rarely do. For example:

s   man   *st*   woman

Also there are no special words for 'the' or 'a' in classical Egyptian and so *s* 'man' can mean either 'a man' or 'the man' (although one or the other often suggests itself in translation into English).

One feature of Egyptian which is rather like English is the use of prepositions (words which are 'pre-posed', or put before, others) to indicate locations ('in'), directions ('towards'), times ('during'), accompaniment ('with') and how things are done ('by'). As in English, the simplest prepositions tend to be very short words and are written with 1-consonant signs:

m   in, with, from, as   *in*   by

⌇ *n*   to(wards) (people), for   *ḥnꜥ*   with

⌒ *r*   to(wards) (place), at

For example:

m pr   in the house   *r pr*   to the house

n snbi for Senbi   *in snbi* by Senbi

§10 Adjectives

An adjective is a word used to describe a noun, to give it a particular property or quality (e.g. 'a **stupid** man', 'a **clever** woman'). The distinctive feature about adjectives in Egyptian is that they *follow* their nouns and also they *agree* with the noun – if the noun is feminine and ends in -*t*, then so does the adjective:

s bin the/an evil man   *st bint* the/an evil woman

The word for 'this' behaves in a similar manner:

pn this (masc.)   *tn* this (fem.)

Like adjectives, *pn* and *tn* follow their noun and agree with it. An example of this occurs in the inscription used at the beginning of this book, where the text ends with the phrase 'this goose':

srw pn   this goose

Exercises

1.1 Kings' names

You are now in a position to read the names of several Old Kingdom kings. First, here is the name of the famous builder of the Great Pyramid of Giza, who is usually known by a Greek adaptation of his name as 'Cheops'. In hieroglyphs his name is written as follows (we have given you a conventional rendering in English afterwards to guide you in your transliteration; for the use of the name-ring or cartouche see p. 20):

. . . . Khufu

Here are two further names of Old Kingdom kings. The first is one of two names of a 5th dynasty king, Djedkare Isesi. Which is given here? The second is a name shared by two kings of the 6th dynasty:

. . . .

1.2 Words from the roasting scene

In the roasting scene used in our introduction, some words are written out with 1-consonant signs. Transliterate the following and see if you can isolate the words in the original scene in §1:

.... roast   .... goose

1.3 Gods' names

The names of certain gods are typically written with 1-consonant signs. Transliterate the following. Once again, the traditional English rendering will help to guide you in most cases (although 'Anubis' is derived from a Greek version of the god's name – 'Inpu' or 'Anpu' might be a more conventional rendering into English). Remember to use the proper transliteration symbols from the second column in the table in §4. Any unfamilar sign (such as the seated dog) is a determinative and so not to be transliterated:

.... Anubis   .... Heket

.... Ptah   .... Sebek or Sobek

.... Ra or Re   .... Seker or Soker

'Sobek' and 'Soker' are usually rendered with an 'o' because of the Greek forms of these names. There is nothing of importance in this traditional practice.

Many readers of this book will be familiar with the famous pharaoh Akhenaten, his wife Nefertiti, and Akhenaten's innovative religious programme centred on the solar disc, the Aten. In hieroglyphs, the Aten is written as follows. Once again, try to transliterate:

.... Aten

'Aten', like 'Anubis', shows the alternative conventional use of 'a' for initial *i* ('Iten' would be the other way of pronouncing this word in English).

1.4 Transliterating words

Transliterate the following words written with 1-consonant signs and determinatives (any sign which is not a 1-consonant sign is a determinative and need not be transliterated):

individual, ordinary man, person   name

festival   bad, evil

bird, fowl   excellent, effective, astute

throwing (the throw stick in fowling scenes)		Poker (place-name, see p. 55)	
staff		go north, go downstream	
sky		fish	
garment		alabaster	
foreleg (joint of meat used in offerings)		shooting, spearing	

1.5 *Writing out words in hieroglyphs*

Write out the following words in hieroglyphs using the determinative supplied. Remember to arrange the hieroglyphs into groups as noted in §5 above:

ḫr   fall   *ḥtm*   (v.) seal, close; (n.) a/the seal

sr   official   *ḳrst*   burial

1.6 *Translation*

Transliterate and translate the following phrases:

a   b

c   d

1.7 *Translating the offering scene*

The scene on p. 12 was used to illustrate the use of hieroglyphs written in right-to-left order in §7 above. Have a go at translating the caption with the help of the vocabulary provided and the ordering of the signs given in §7. (The context of the scene is that the figure is offering the foreleg of a slaughtered bull to the tomb owner Senbi; the inscription relates his speech.) This exercise is useful in illustrating a couple of other points as well. First, these are drawings of real hieroglyphs found on the wall of the tomb of Senbi and not the standard hieroglyphs of a font such as that used in this book (recall how English written letters differ a little from standard type fonts). This is really just a matter of getting used to variability, particularly in the infill of signs – use the vocabulary provided to see the standard hieroglyphs. Secondly, the inscription contains words written in other ways than with 1-consonant signs which you will not be able to read through at present. Instead, use a 'cut-and-paste' approach, relying on us to isolate the correct groups of hieroglyphs in the vocabulary and to give their correct reading and meaning. You should just 'cut-and-paste' the relevant groups into your translations. By the end of the next chapter, even these words should be clear to you.

VOCABULARY

	mꜣꜥ-ḫrw	the justified		*n kꜣ n*	for the ka of
	ḫpš	foreleg (of ox used in offering)		*snbi*	Senbi (name)

(*mꜣꜥ-ḫrw* is used like our own R.I.P as a phrase referring to the blessed dead; offerings are made to the ka-spirit of the deceased.)

   Note the interaction of art and text in this example, where the foreleg is an integral part of the scene, but also serves as the determinative of the word *ḫpš* (it can be 'read' at the correct point of the inscription at the end of the word for foreleg).

   This inscription comes from the Middle Kingdom tombs at Meir, the cemetery site for Qis, the principal town of the 14th Upper Egyptian nome (province). We shall make use of these tombs, particularly that of the governor Senbi, for scenes to supplement your study of the Middle Kingdom stelae in the British Museum.

1.8 Study exercise: A fishing and fowling scene
Transliterate and translate the labels above the scene on p. 14 using the vocabulary and notes below the picture.

Fishing and fowling scene from the tomb of Senbi at Meir (Meir I, pl. 2). The hieroglyphs have been edited to fit the content of Chapter 1. The scene is studied with its original inscriptions in Exercise 4.6.

Notes

i The words for 'birds' and 'fish' are given in an abbreviated form rather than being written out fully. They are still the same two words (in the plural) as the words given in Exercise 1.4.

ii *mꜣꜥ-ḫrw* 'the justified' has now been given in three different writings (see vocabulary Exercise 1.7). Such variations in the 'spelling' of words will be explained in the next chapter.

VOCABULARY

ꜣpd(w)	fowl, birds	
ỉn	in	by
ꜥmꜣ	throwing	
mꜣꜥ-ḫrw	the justified	
r	at, towards	
rm(w)	fish	
snbỉ	Senbi	
stt	spearing	

More uses of hieroglyphs

The aim of this chapter is to introduce you to the 2-consonant and 3-consonant signs, which provide much of the subtlety and flexibility of the hieroglyphic script. It will also supply you with the information needed to read the names of various famous kings of ancient Egypt, including the names on the Abydos king-list in the British Museum.

§11 2-consonant signs

The second major group of signs are the 2-consonant signs, which contribute two consonants to the reading of a word. We have already seen an example in the use of the 2-consonant sign ☐ *pr* in the word ☐ ⅄ *pr* 'go (out)'. The 2-consonant signs are rather common – over eighty are used in this book – and becoming familiar with them represents the major hurdle to be overcome in reading hieroglyphs. The sign-list on p. 128 gives a table of the most common 2-consonant signs used in the inscriptions studied, and we shall also introduce several at a time in the vocabularies to the various exercises to allow you to become familiar with them in convenient numbers. The following are some common examples of 2-consonant signs to get you started, along with some common words in which they occur (including *pr* again so that you can see how the table works):

SIGN		EXAMPLE		SIGN		EXAMPLE	
⟜	*ꜥ3*		*ꜥ3*	great, large		*b3*		*b3k*	servant
	wr		*wr*	great, important		*mr*		*mr*	love, want
	nb		*nb*	lord, master		*pr*		*pr*	go out
	ḥs		*ḥs*	praise, favour		*ḥ3*		*ḥ3*	thousand

Consider the word *b3k* 'servant'. In its most basic form, the word is built up through using the 2-consonant sign 🦆 *b3* followed by the 1-consonant sign ⌢ *k*, which together give the reading of the word as *b3k* (it may also be finished off by a seated man determinative – see §6 above – showing us that the word refers to a person). Notice how this gives a more visually distinctive writing for the word than if it were simply written out with 1-consonant signs. Although we might view the number of 2-consonant signs as rather forbidding, it is nothing compared to the enormous number of words which any language contains. By having a mixed system in which they can be written with differing combinations of hieroglyphs, words take on more distinctive and memorable writings than if they were simply written out in an alphabet-like system (think of the difficulties of English spelling!).

The second noticeable point in the writing of some of these words is that 1-consonant signs often occur as *sound complements* fleshing out the reading of a 2-consonant sign, helping to jog the memory, as it were, about its reading. There is a simple rule about this: if a 1-consonant sign shares the same value as an accompanying 2-consonant sign, then this 1-consonant sign is not read as a separate sound. So, if we look at ⬚⌒ again, we read *pr* and not *prr* even though it is written with ⬚ *pr* + ⌒ *r*, because ⌒ *r* jogs our memory about the *r* of *pr*.

If, however, the 1-consonant sign has a different value from the sounds of an accompanying 2-consonant sign, then it should be read as a separate sound. So, if we look at the word 🐦🏠 *bꜣk*, then the 1-consonant sign ⌒ *k* must be read separately, since the sign 🐦 only reads *bꜣ* on its own. So read *bꜣk*.

From our point of view, this might seem an unnecessarily complex way to go about writing words, but there are a number of advantages. For example, such a system provides the flexibility to be able to write words in blocks as noted in §5. More importantly, it allows a good deal of flexibility in the actual choice of signs used; this was particularly useful in view of the fact that most hieroglyphic inscriptions were written on fixed and inflexible surfaces such as stone.

Suppose that we have two inscriptions, each with a different-sized space left at the end of a line, and we wish to write the word *bꜣk* 'servant' in each of these spaces. The hieroglyphic system allows us a convenient and elegant way out of our problem. In the smaller space we can write *bꜣk* as it is written in the table above: 🐦🏠 . In the larger space, we could include a sound-complement 🦅 fleshing out the *ꜣ* of the *bꜣ*-sign and thus fill the slightly larger space: 🐦🦅🏠 .

The two words read just the same, they are just 'spelt out' slightly differently. Words in hieroglyphic writing, therefore, do not have one single correct spelling but are rather 'elastic' and can be contracted or expanded through, for example, the inclusion or omission of sound-complements. Fortunately, we can leave it to the ancient Egyptians to do all the spelling for us – the important point for us is just to be aware of the flexibility of the script and observe it in action.

§12 3-consonant signs

The final major group of sound-signs are the 3-consonant signs, which contribute three consonants to the reading of a word. 3-consonant signs are also often accompanied by one or two 1-consonant signs as sound complements helping to flesh out the reading of the sign. There are far fewer of these signs and also many of them are emblematic – they are used only in certain words and are often connected to, or come to be emblems for, the words in which they are used. Perhaps the most famous example of these signs is ☥ *ꜥnḫ*, 'ankh', used in the word for 'life':

SIGN		EXAMPLE			SIGN		EXAMPLE		
☥	*ꜥnḫ*	☥	*ꜥnḫ*	life		*wsr*		*wsr*	strong, powerful
	nfr		*nfr*	good		*nṯr*		*nṯr*	god
	ḥtp		*ḥtp*	rest, satisfy		*ḫpr*		*ḫpr*	become
	mꜣꜥ		*mꜣꜥ*	true, right, proper		*ḫrw*		*ḫrw*	voice

The two words *mꜣꜥ* and *ḫrw* have already been met in the phrase *mꜣꜥ-ḫrw* 'true of voice' or 'justified'. This, as already noted, is a common epithet bestowed on the blessed dead (whose conduct has been judged before the gods to be true) and is used after the names of the deceased in a similar manner to our R.I.P. (⟍ is a 2-consonant sign reading *mꜣ*):

mꜣꜥ-ḫrw   true of voice, justified

You have encountered this in more condensed writings. (See further §14 on p. 18 below.)

§13 Ideograms: sound-meaning signs

The final signs to be looked at in this chapter are the sound-meaning signs (ideograms) which combine sound and meaning and which come closest to our own preconceptions of how a picture-script should work:

	ib	heart		*r*	mouth
	ꜥ	arm		*rꜥ*	the sun
	pr	house		*ḥr*	face

As the examples indicate, these signs are often followed by ı which helps to highlight the ideogram usage, as well as noting that only one 'heart' etc. is meant; it also serves as a space filler to give a convenient grouping of the signs. A fuller list of ideograms is given on pp. 128-129.

Sound-meaning signs can be accompanied by sound complements or determinatives:

𓎝	*w'b*	pure, priest		𓆳	*rnpt*	year
𓄿𓄓	*sḏm*	hear		𓏏𓈇	*tꜣ*	land

This usage of signs illustrates an important point for using this book. Although you may be able to 'spell out' a couple of the words given in this section, most of them will not be immediately readable (you should, however, rapidly grow used to reading 𓎝 as *w'b*, for example). Therefore we encourage you to focus on words as a whole, rather than trying to puzzle through the use of every single sign from first principles. We will do the work for you by supplying you with words in the format used in the table above: hieroglyphic writing followed by transliteration and translation. If you concentrate on whole words as opposed to single signs, you should find that you make faster progress in reading.

§14 Variant writings

Hieroglyphs are written in groups, accommodating aesthetic considerations and the limits of physical space by using differing combinations of signs. For these reasons, words can be written in a number of different ways. For example, we have already encountered the phrase *mꜣ'-ḥrw* 'true of voice' or 'justified' in a number of different writings:

As already noted, we can safely leave it to the ancient Egyptians to show us how it should be done. We need only be aware that variant spelling is a perfectly normal feature of hieroglyphic writing.

However, it is worth noting that 'spelling' is constrained by convention and tradition within fairly strict limits. So, even though *mꜣ'-ḥrw* is written out in a number of different ways, there are usually distinctive and recognisable elements to the phrase (in this case ═ and 𓏺). Furthermore, by tradition, *mꜣ'* is never found written out with 1-consonant signs as * 𓄿𓄿═ *mꜣ'* (* is the symbol for 'not found'); rather the range of 'spelling' of *mꜣ'* concerns whether ═ *mꜣ'* was written along with 𓄿 *mꜣ* as a sound complement (often combined into 𓄿═), and perhaps also with other sound complements in differing combinations, to suit aesthetic and physical considerations.

§15 Writing the plural (see also Reference table on p. 149)
The most common way of writing the plural has already been discussed in §8 above. It is typically written with plural strokes (ı ı ı) and may or may not show a -*w* sound-sign (in the latter case, a *w* is added to the transliteration in brackets for convenience):

$$\text{𓎛𓃀𓋴𓂝𓏥 or 𓎛𓃀𓋴𓏥}\qquad \textit{ḥbsw or ḥbs(w)}\qquad \text{clothes}$$

Another way of writing the plural is for a sign to be repeated three times:

$$\text{𓏤𓏤𓏤}\qquad \textit{t3(w)}\quad \text{lands}$$

This method is rarer in practice, although it is favoured for certain words, such as *t3(w)* 'lands'.

Egyptian also shows a restricted use of a dual ending: msc. ꜥ\\ -*wy* and fem. ◠\\ -*ty* (indicating two of something), but this is common only with things which tend to come in pairs:

𓂝𓏤𓃀\\ *ꜥwy* arms   𓇾𓇾 *t3wy* the two lands (Egypt: Delta and Valley)

t3wy is written by repeating two signs, like the second plural method noted above.

§16 ◠ *nb* 'all, every, any' and ◠ *nb* 'lord, master'
There are two important words which can be written alike. The first is the word for 'all', 'every' or 'any':

◠   *nb*   all, every, any

◠ *nb* 'all, every, any', behaves rather like an adjective (see §10): it *follows* the noun it goes with and, like an adjective, agrees with it:

𓐍𓏏𓎟   *ḫt nbt*   everything

◠ also occurs in another common word, the word *nb* meaning 'lord' or 'master', which, in its most abbreviated form, is written simply:

◠   *nb*   lord, master

Fortunately, when *nb* means 'lord' or 'master' it comes first in expressions:

◠𓃀𓇩   *nb 3bḏw*   lord of Abydos

(See Exercise 2.2 for *3bḏw* 'Abydos'.)

So the rule is quite simple: when *nb* comes second in its phrase (and agrees with the first noun) then it is the word *nb* 'all, every, any'; when it comes first in its phrase, it is the word *nb* 'lord, master'.

§17 Royal names and titles

One of the principal goals of this chapter is to equip you to read the names of the kings of Egypt. In the next few paragraphs, we will deal with some of the background about royal names, focusing on the titles, epithets and the dating formula. In the Exercises to this chapter, we shall set you loose on the names of the kings themselves.

The king in ancient Egypt had an elaborate titulary made up of his names, titles and epithets. From the Old Kingdom onwards, each king had five names, of which three are particularly common on monuments (the other two – the 'two ladies' and the 'golden Horus' names – are used less often). The three common names are the Horus name and the names contained in cartouches – the praenomen and the nomen.

The *Horus name* designates the king as the god Horus, the son and successor of Osiris (for whom, see pp. 40-42). The name is introduced by the falcon 𓅃 *ḥr*. As an example the Horus name of Senwosret I is:

𓅃𓋹𓏠𓋴   *ḥr ꜥnḫ-mswt*   the Horus Ankhmesut

The other two common names are written in cartouches (name-rings). The *praenomen*, or first cartouche-name (a name assigned on the king's accession), follows the 𓇓𓏏 *nsw-bity* title 'king of the dualities', 'dual king' – i.e. the king as ruler of the dualities which composed the Egyptian world: Upper and Lower Egypt; desert and cultivation; the human and the divine. It has been traditional to focus on the division of Egypt into the Nile Valley and the Delta and to translate this title as 'king of Upper and Lower Egypt'. The praenomen of Senwosret I is:

𓇓𓏏𓆥(𓇳𓆣𓂓)   *nsw-bity ḫpr-kꜣ-rꜥ*   the king of Upper and Lower Egypt Kheperkare

The *nomen*, or second cartouche-name, is the king's own birth name and might be common to other members of the dynasty. It is also the name by which scholars nowadays refer to the kings: hence we have Senwosret I, II, and III in the 12th dynasty. The numbers are a modern convention and do not occur in the ancient names. The nomen is typically introduced by the 𓇅𓅆 *sꜣ rꜥ* title 'son of Re' – i.e. the king as the heir of the sun-god Re on earth. The nomen of Senwosret I is:

𓇅𓇳(𓇳𓍿𓈖𓄗)   *sꜣ rꜥ s-n-wsrt*   son of Re Senwosret

(See Exercise 2.7 on pp. 26-27 for the readings of the cartouche names themselves, and the ordering of the signs.)

A couple of other titles of the king (typically accompanying the praenomen) are:

ntr nfr   the perfect god   nb tзwy   lord of the two lands

§18 Royal epithets

The king's name and titles are usually associated with a number of epithets. Among the most common are epithets connected with life:

ʿnḫ ḏt   living enduringly   di ʿnḫ   given life

often extended:

mi rʿ   like Re   ḏt r nḥḥ   enduringly and repeatedly (for ever and eternity)

On the written order of the phrase *mi rʿ* 'like Re', you may wish to look ahead to §22 in the next chapter.

§19 Dating

Dates were recorded in ancient Egypt according to the regnal year of the reigning king and not by some absolute dating system like BC/AD. The dating formula has a fixed and regular form based around the following words, along with the names, titles and epithets of the king and the number of years of his reign:

rnpt-sp   regnal year   ḥr   under

ḥm   person   n   of

ḥm is used to refer indirectly to the king.

Egyptian numbering is decimal, broken up into tens and units. The tens are reckoned by repetition of the sign ∩ (so ∩∩∩ = 30) and the units by repetition of I (so IIII = 4). Consider the following example (here year 28 of king Nimaatre Amenemhet III) which shows how the formula is put together and how the numbering system works:

The date in the lunette of BM EA 827:

BM EA 827:   *rnpt-sp 28 ḥr ḥm n nsw-bity (n)-mзʿt-rʿ ʿnḫ ḏt*
             Regnal year 28 under the person of the king of Upper and Lower Egypt Nimaatre living enduringly

(On the title and epithets of the king, see the previous paragraphs. On the cartouche name of the king himself, see Exercise 2.7 on pp. 26-27. The *n* of Nimaatre was omitted in the original.)

Excursus: chart of royal dynasties

Kings of Egypt prior to the invasion by Alexander the Great(332 BC) are organised by scholars into thirty dynasties, further arranged into major periods known as Kingdoms (normally when only one king at a time ruled Egypt) and Intermediate Periods (when the kingship was often divided). This book principally concerns monuments from the First Intermediate Period and Middle Kingdom (*c.*2150 BC–*c.*1641 BC), but the kings listed below are discussed on pp. 26-31.

Archaic Period Dynasties 1-2	
2500 BC	
Old Kingdom Dynasties 3-6	**12th Dynasty (c.1937–1759 BC)** Sehetepibre Amenemhet (I) Kheperkare Senwosret (I) Nubkaure Amenemhet (II) Khakheperre Senwosret (II) Khakaure Senwosret (III) Nimaatre Amenemhet (III) Maakherure Amenemhet (IV) Sobekkare Nefrusobek
2000 BC 1st Intermediate Period Dynasties 7-10 Middle Kingdom Dynasties 11-13	
2nd Intermediate Period Dynasties 14-17 **1500 BC**	**18th Dynasty (c.1539–1295 BC)** Nebpehtyre Ahmose Djeserkare Amenhotep (I) Aakheperkare Thutmose (I) Aakheperenre Thutmose (II) Menkheperre Thutmose (III) Maatkare Hatshepsut-khenmetamun Aakheperure Amenhotep (II) Menkheperure Thutmose (IV) Nebmaatre Amenhotep (III) Neferkheperure-waenre Akhenaten Ankhkheperure Smenkhkare Nebkheperure Tutankhamun-hekaiunushema Kheperkheperure Itnetjer-Ay Djeserkheperure-setepenre Horemheb-meryamun
New Kingdom Dynasties 18-20	
1000 BC 3rd Intermediate Period Dynasties 21-25	
500 BC Late Period Dynasties 26-30	
	19th Dynasty (c.1295–1186 BC) Menpehtyre Ramesse (I) Menmaatre Sety (I) Usermaatre-setepenre Ramesse-meryamun (II)
BC **AD**	

Note: all dates are approximate; you will find slightly different schemes used in different books.

Exercises

2.1 Signs

The following are a list of signs to be used in the Exercises. They are worth memorising (writing them out is a good way of familiarising yourself with them).

a. 2-consonant signs

Some of these sign occur in the word exercises below; others will be of use when studying kings' names in Exercises 2.7 and 2.8:

	ꜣb or *mr*		*wp*		*mr*		*nb*		*kꜣ*
or	*ꜥꜣ*		*mꜣ*		*mr*		*ḥꜥ*		*ḏw*
	wꜣ		*mn*		*ms*		*sꜣ*		*ḏd*

b. 3-consonant signs

The following 3-consonant signs were introduced in the main text above. Write out and learn these signs and the following common words they occur in, using the opportunity to follow the use of sound-complements and determinatives.

ꜥnḫ	*ꜥnḫ*	life		*wsr*		*wsr*	powerful
nfr	*nfr*	good		*nṯr*		*nṯr*	god
ḥtp	*ḥtp*	rest, satisfy		*ḫpr*		*ḫpr*	become

A further useful 3-consonant sign is: *ẖnm*

c. Ideograms

	SIGN		EXAMPLE
	A55, vase with water flowing, combined with leg		*wꜥb* pure
	C9, flat alluvial land with grains of sand		*tꜣ* land
	F42, road bordered by shrubs		*wꜣt* road, way

To aid you in further study, these signs have been quoted with their classification (composed of a letter and a number) as found in the sign-list on pp. 129–143.

Note: ⸗ often occurs without the grains of sand as ⸗ (C10) alone.

2.2 Words

a. Copy out and transliterate the following words (you may wish to refer to the list of signs above or the sign-tables at the end of the book):

🦆🐦 or 🦆	.... son	🪣 or 🪣	.... ka (the spirit of sustenance)

Since both of these common words rely on a single 2-consonant sign, it is not at all unusual to find them written at their briefest with just the 2-consonant sign.

🦅🐾	.... road, way	🪶🐦	.... love, wish, want, desire
𓏏🐾	.... companion	🪣	.... open, separate

(Notice that in the word for 'road', 'way', 🚏 can be used as a determinative with the word 'spelt out', or as an ideogram as in Exercise 2.1.)

b. Two important town-sites which occur in common epithets of the god Osiris are:

🪶🪣	.... Abydos	🪶🐦	.... Djedu (Busiris)

c. Some more names of gods:

🪶	.... Amun	🐦🐍	.... Khnum

Try and transliterate the name of the god Wepwawet (you may need to consult §15 again):

🐾 .... Wepwawet

The names of these gods can be written with or without the determinative for gods: 🪶 (A3).

2.3 Variant writings

In §14 in the text, you were introduced to the notion of variant writings, which allow a word to be stretched or compressed to fit space. The example used was the phrase *mȝꜥ-ḥrw* 'justified' or 'true of voice', used as an epithet of the blessed dead. The variants given in previous examples are repeated here. Work through the writings, identifying the various signs, and satisfying yourself that despite the differences, they all yield the same transliteration: *mȝꜥ-ḥrw*.

2.4 Expressions

Transliterate and translate the following phrases (both of which are common elements of the offering formula which you will study in more depth in Chapter 3):

a. 𓏺𓀀   b. 𓇋𓏏𓆑𓊃𓅱𓈖

As so often, the same phrase can be written in a more condensed manner (although it is read in the same way), for example:

𓇋𓏏𓆑𓅱

(You may wish to consult §§9 and 10 on nouns and adjectives in Egyptian.)

2.5 Words

Some very common words are written with otherwise uncommon signs and with some idiosyncracies of their own. Copy out the following and read the accompanying notes:

𓇋𓏏𓀀 or 𓏏	*it*	father	It seems that ⌣ is an obscure determinative here; however, the common phrase *it=f* 'his father' is probably influential too (cf. §§33, 36).
𓊨 or 𓊨𓁹	*3sir*	Osiris	Written with E60-seat above A36-eye for reasons which are still obscure. *3sir* is a recently suggested reading (rather than older *wsir*)
𓏏𓏥	*t*	bread	Written with D25 and F9 or F10-bread determinatives and plural strokes. In offering formulae it is often abbreviated to 𓏏.

2.6 Dating

The following are examples of dates from British Museum stelae. It is perhaps better to do this exercise after the study exercises on pp. 26-30, when you will be able to read the kings' names more easily.

The lunette of the round-topped stela of Senwosretsenbu (BM EA 557) begins:

BM EA 557:   𓄤𓍿𓈖𓈖𓈖𓎛𓇓𓅱𓏏𓇓𓏠𓈖𓏏𓀭𓂝𓈖𓐍

In the first line of BM EA 586 the king's cartouche is surmounted by the sky hieroglyph, which is not read:

BM EA 586,
Line 1:

BM EA 567 begins with a date; the writing of nsw-bity is to fit the rounded shape:

BM EA 567,
Lines 1-2:

2.7 *Study exercise: Middle Kingdom kings of the 12th dynasty*

It is now time for you to read through the cartouche names of various kings of Egypt. The kings we have selected come from the some of the most celebrated dynasties of ancient Egypt: the 12th dynasty in the Middle Kingdom, and the 18th, 19th and 20th dynasties in the New Kingdom. You can either piece their names together from the sign resources provided below or you can go further and refer back to Chapters 1 and 2 (as well as making use of the sign-tables at the end of the book) to improve your familiarity with the signs.

The two most common names of the king – the praenomen and nomen – are written in cartouches and are thus easy to spot. However, the way that the names themselves are written is actually surprisingly complex, playing with the various resources of the script for aesthetic and spacing reasons. The one factor we have not covered so far (because it finds a more appropriate place in Chapter 3) is that elements drawing on divine names are written first, regardless of the order in which they are read. For example, the sun-disc *rˁ* (the name of the sun god) regularly appears first in the praenomen but is read last (as the transliteration values and Anglicisation of the names below show). For the purposes of this exercise, we would ask you to follow the reading order we give below, but you may wish to look forward to §22 in Chapter 3 for an account of this peculiarity.

Fill in the first cartouche names from the list below into the proper place in the following table (the first one is done for you). Notice, once again, that the element *rˁ* is written before the other elements of the name (similarly with *wsrt* in *s-n-wsrt*), although it is not read first:

Sehetepibre	*sḥtp-ib-rˁ*		
Amenemhet (I)	*imn-m-ḥ3t*		
. . . .	. . . .		
Senwosret (I)	*s-n-wsrt*		
. . . .	. . . .		
Amenemhet (II)	*imn-m-ḥ3t*		

. . . . Senwosret (II)	. . . . *s-n-wsrt*		
. . . . Senwosret (III)	. . . . *s-n-wsrt*		
. . . . Amenemhet (III)	. . . . *imn-m-ḥȝt*		
. . . . Amenemhet (IV)	. . . . *imn-m-ḥȝt*		
. . . . Nefrusobek	. . . . *nfrw-sbk*		

List of first-cartouche names (in jumbled order):

ḫˤ-kȝw-rˤ Khakaure	*ḫˤ-ḫpr-rˤ* Khakheperre	*ḫpr-kȝ-rˤ* Kheperkare	*mȝˤ-ḫrw-rˤ* Maakherure
n-mȝˤt-rˤ Nimaatre	*nbw-kȝw-rˤ* Nubkaure	*sḥtp-ib-rˤ* Sehetepibre	*sbk-kȝ-rˤ* Sobekkare

SIGNS

	ib	*ib* heart		*imn*	*amun/amen-* (the god) Amun
	wsrt	*wosret* the powerful one		*m*	*em* in
	mȝˤ	*maa* truc		*mȝˤt*	*maat* (the goddess) Maat (truth)
	n	*en* or *ni* of		*nbw*	*nub* gold
	nfrw	*nefru* beauty		*ḥȝt*	*het/hat* (fore)front
	ḫˤ	*kha* appear(ance)		*ḫpr*	*kheper* being/form
	ḫrw	*kheru* voice		*s*	*s(e)* man
or	*sbk*	*sebek/sobek* (the god) Sobek		*sḥtp*	*sehetep* make satisifed
	kȝ	*ka* the ka-spirit		*kȝw*	*kau* the ka-spirits

All the first cartouche names contain the following element:

⊙   *rꜥ*   *ra* or *re*
(the god) Re (or Ra)

Many of these elements have proper meaning as words on their own, which we indicate here. However, there is no need to try and translate the names.

2.8 Study exercise: New Kingdom kings

Transliterate both the cartouche names for each of the following New King-dom kings, using the aids provided. A complicating factor is that, during the New Kingdom, it is not at all uncommon to find epithets included within royal cartouches. Some of the names below contain such epithets (for example that of the ruling queen Hatshepsut, which regularly includes the epithet *ḥnmt-imn* – 'joined with (the god) Amun'). If the epithet contains the name of a god, this divine element may be written at the front of the cartouche, even if it is not read first. Follow the lead given in the Anglicised versions of the names below:

Nebpehtyre
Ahmose

Djeserkare
Amenhotep (I)

Aakheperkare
Thutmose (I)

Aakheperenre
Thutmose (II)

Maatkare
Hatshepsut-khenmetamun

Menkheperre
Thutmose (III)

Aakheperure
Amenhotep hekaiunu (II)

Menkheperure
Thutmose (IV)

Nebmaatre
Amenhotep hekawaset (III)

Neferkheprure-waenre
Akhenaten

Nebkheperure
Tutankhamen-hekaiunushema

Djeserkheperure-setepenre
Horemheb-meryamun

Menpehtyre Ramesse (I)		
Menmaatre Sety-meryenptah (I)		
Usermaatre-setepenre Ramesse-meryamun (II)		
Usermaatre-meryamun Ramesse-hekaiunu (III)		

VOCABULARY

	ȝḫ	*akh* spirit		*iʿḥ*	*(i)ah* moon-god
	iwnw	*iunu* Heliopolis	or	*imn*	*amun/amen-* (the god) Amun
	itn	*aten* Aten (solar disc)	or	*ʿȝ*	*aa* great
	ʿnḫ	*ankh* life/living		*wʿ*	*wa* the (sole) one
	wȝst	*waset* Thebes (place-name)		*wsr*	*weser/user* powerful
	pḥtt for *pḥty*	*pehty* strength		*ptḥ*	*ptah* (the god) Ptah
	m	*em* in		*mȝʿt*	*maat* Maat (truth)
	mn	*men* established	or ... or	*mry*	*mery* beloved
	ms	*mose* bear, form		*n*	*en* of
	nb	*neb* lord		*nfr*	*nefer* perfect
or	*rʿ*	*re/ra* (the god) Re		*ḥȝt*	*hat* front, first
	ḥb	*heb* festival		*ḥr*	*hor* (the god) Horus
	ḥkȝ	*heka* ruler	or	*ḥtp*	*hetep/hotep* satisfied
	ḫpr	*kheper* being/form		*ḫprw*	*kheperu* beings/forms
	ḫnmt	*khenmet* joined (with)	or	*sw, s(w)*	*su, se* him

VOCABULARY (CONTINUED)

𓊃𓏭𓏏	*sty*	*Sety* Sety, i.e. man of (the god) Seth	𓇉	*stp*	*setep* chosen
𓀻	*špswt*	*shepsut* distinguished women	𓇌	*šmꜥ*	*shema* southern
𓂓	*kꜣ*	*ka* the ka-spirit	𓌒	*twt*	*tut* image
𓅝	*ḏḥwty*	*Thut-* (the god) Thoth	𓎛	*ḏsr*	*djeser* sacred/holy

2.9 Study exercise: BM EA 117 (the Abydos king-list of Ramesses II)

The 'king-list' of Ramesses II shown on p. 31 originally came from his temple at Abydos. Modelled on a similar list in his father Seti I's mortuary temple nearby, the list forms part of an elaborate offering formula (*ḥtp-di-nsw*; see Chapter 3) for the cult of previous kings. Originally, there were 78 cartouches in the upper registers (the 76 found in the Seti I list plus the two cartouche names of Ramesses II). This number probably reflects cultic tradition, the space available on the wall, and possibly the 76 forms of the sun-god enumerated in the religious text known as the Litany of Re. The kings are identified by praenomen beneath which are determinatives of seated kings alternately wearing the white 𓋇 and red 𓋌 crowns. The names of Ramesses II (alternating between nomen and praenomen) are repeated in the bottom register and show a range of variant writings for the nomen. Reconstructing the top line from the Seti I king-list, the overall format is as follows:

[An offering which the king gives before Ptah-Sokar-Osiris ... a thousand bread and beer, etc.] to king X as a gift of Ramesses II:

𓈖𓇓	*n nsw*	for the king
𓂝𓂋𓂝	*m ḏd*	as a gift of (literally, in the giving of)

The word *nsw* is written using 𓇓 which is also a variant for 𓈖 common in the New Kingdom (compare the more usual spelling of *nsw* in §23).

The king-list shows some interesting gaps between the Middle and New Kingdom (between the fourth and fifth cartouches of the second surviving register) and within the 18th dynasty. Use the royal names listed in the previous Exercises and the chart of royal dynasties on p. 22 to identify the missing kings and dynasties for yourself.

BM EA 117 (The Abydos king-list of Ramesses II)
(carved and painted limestone; H. 135cm)

Chapter 3

Special writings

In this chapter we introduce you to a number of special writings: abbreviations, changes in the order of signs and defective writings. Since all of these are rather common, particularly in the rendering of titles and epithets, a knowledge of them is essential for successful monument reading in a museum. You are also introduced to the offering formula, probably the most common form of hieroglyphic inscription to be found on funerary monuments surviving from ancient Egypt. This chapter should also serve as a convenient reference resource to which you can return when studying various monuments later on in the book.

§20 Abbreviations

Abbreviated writings are common in the writing of titles and epithets:

      ḥ3ty-ʿ   governor, mayor   *ḥry-ḥbt*   lector priest

ḥ3ty-ʿ (literally, 'foremost of position') is written with the ideogram *ḥ3t* (front part of lion) over ⎯ʿ (arm); *ḥry-ḥbt* (literally, 'the carrier of the book of ritual') is written with abbreviated writings of both *ḥry* and *ḥbt* (without sound complements or determinatives). There is also graphic transposition, with the two tall signs placed either side of *ḥr(y)* (see §21 below). Clearly such writings cannot be read sign by sign with any ease. Even after more than a century and a half of study, the exact reading of some words remains contentious among Egyptologists! Hence we strongly recommend that you follow our general advice of concentrating on whole words rather than getting bogged down in the study of individual signs.

     As we have already seen, abbreviated writings of the epithet usually bestowed on the blessed dead are common:

      m3ʿ-ḥrw   written in full as: true of voice, justified

§21 Change of order: spacing

The second feature is the switching of the order of signs to enable them to fit into the available space in a more satisfactory manner (termed more formally *graphic transposition*):

      instead of   *ḏdw*   Djedu

Graphic transposition also occurs in vertical columns:

   ḏdw Djedu, instead of

Sometimes graphic transposition is a regular feature of the writing of a word:

m33   see, look at

This is regularly written with the determinative ⌒ placed under the 2-consonant sign ⟋ *m3*.

§22 Change of order: prestige

For reasons of prestige, names for gods and kings and related words sometimes precede closely connected words, although they are actually read afterwards (this is termed more formally *honorific transposition*). Honorific transposition is particularly common in epithets and titles:

rḫ nsw	king's advisor, royal intimate	
mry imn	beloved of Amun	
ḥm-nṯr	servant of the god, priest	
mi rꜥ	like Re	

(Notice that abbreviated writings are also common.)

You have already encountered this phenomenon in the writing of royal names in Exercises 2.7 and 2.8. A rather dramatic illustration of this point is the following writing of the nomen of Ramesses II (Ramesse-meryamun, 'Ramesses beloved of Amun'):

Here the two divine elements (Ra of the name Ramesses and Amun of the epithet 'beloved of Amun') have been written as seated gods and placed at the top of the cartouche facing each other, creating a vertical division. The low flat sign of *mr(y)* ('beloved') has been placed in the middle of the cartouche, creating a horizontal division. The vertical division is mirrored in the bottom half of the cartouche (giving the *ms-sw* or 'messe' part of Ramesses) where the three-pronged *ms*-sign stands in the centre between two tall thin signs (the *sw* and the *s*) both of which bend away at the top from the central *ms*-sign.

§23 Defective or strange writings

A few common words are written without the full set of sound-signs, probably for reasons of grouping; *nsw* 'king' is written in an unusual manner:

[glyph]	*r(m)t*	people	[glyph]	*ḥ(n)ḳt*	beer
[glyph]	*s(my)t*	desert	[glyph]	*nsw*	king

§24 Titles

Office-holding played a central role in the élite culture of ancient Egypt, locating the individual within society, most notably in relation to the king (see also pp. 101-104). Titles come in two forms: official or administrative titles and conventional titles connected with status and authority. Abbreviated writings are common to both.

a. Conventional titles of status and authority

The two most common conventional titles are:

[glyph]	*ḫtmty bity*	seal-bearer of the king	[glyph]	*smr wˁt(y)*	sole companion

(The reading of *ḫtmty-bity* is unsure: other possibilities are *ḫtmw-bity* and *sḏꜣwty-bity*; for *bity* 'king', see p. 102.) These two titles often occur together.

b. Titles of office

Titles of office can be divided into secular and religious titles:

Secular titles

[glyph]	*ḥꜣty-ˁ*	governor, mayor	[glyph]	*m-r ˁḫnwty*	overseer of the chamber

A number of titles are composed with the element [glyph] *m-r* (fully *imy-r*) 'overseer':

[glyph]	*m-r pr*	steward, overseer of the estate	[glyph]	*m-r mšˁ*	overseer of the army

m-r probably means literally 'the one in whom is the word' (i.e. the one who has the authority to issue orders). On the basis of a graphic pun around *r* (which means both 'mouth' and 'word'), it is occasionally written with [glyph] B44 tongue (the tongue being 'the one in the mouth'):

[glyph]	*m-r pr*	steward

Religious titles

𓊹𓈖𓈖𓈖𓀀	wʿb	priest (literally, pure one)	𓍛𓊹	ḥm-nṯr	priest (literally, servant of the god)
𓊪𓂋𓐍𓋴	ḥry-sštꜣ	master of secrets	𓏲𓎛𓃀	ḥry-ḥbt	lector priest

It is not at all uncommon for titles to be written without determinatives.

§25 Epithets

Egyptian texts abound with epithets of gods, kings and officials. Here are a couple of related epithets particularly common on stelae:

𓄪𓏭𓏭 or 𓄪 or 𓇋𓄪𓅱	imꜣḫy or imꜣḫw	venerable one, revered one, honourable one
𓎟𓄪	nb imꜣḫ	possessor of veneration/reverence

and other variants based on the fuller writings such as: 𓇋𓄿𓄪 'reverence', 'veneration'.

These epithets are primarily applied to the blessed dead. After a life of official duty and ethical behaviour, the blessed dead were revered by the living (who perpetuate their memory on earth, particularly through offerings) and honoured before the gods (with whom they exist beyond death as transfigured spirits). The latter is often expressed in the following way:

𓇋𓄪𓏭𓏭𓏤𓁹	imꜣḫy ḫr ꜣsir	the revered one before Osiris

§26 The offering formula

Formulae comprise relatively fixed combinations of words and so can be read without a detailed understanding of their internal grammar. The most common example, the offering formula, is a ubiquitous feature of the hieroglyphic monuments found in museums throughout the world. By working through, and becoming familiar with, the elements of the formula discussed below, you will gain access to a vast number of hieroglyphic inscriptions.

The offering formula merges two related functions: official and personal. In official terms, the status of the deceased as one of the blessed dead was linked to the successful performance of official functions in royal service and ethical behaviour in life. This success was instrumental in qualifying the deceased for access to the means of commemoration in terms of memorial inscriptions and funerary monuments. One purpose of the offering formula was to allow the deceased to partake of the offerings presented to the deities in the major cult temples in the name of the king, particularly on festival occasions. This reversion of offerings displays the importance of official life, particularly in terms of the person of the king, in the relationship between the living and the dead.

The second, personal, function relates more to the private family-based aspects of the funerary cult of the deceased. The private offerings to the dead could be either physical (the offering of food, drink and goods) or verbal (through the utterance of the offering formula); furthermore, these offerings could be perpetuated in pictorial and verbal form (through art and writing). In this way, the offerings made at the burial could be perpetuated by family members (particularly the son and heir), or by people visiting the tomb or passing by the stela.

First of all, here is an example of the offering formula, which you may wish to refer back to as you read over the discussion below:

The offering formula from BM EA 558:

Hieroglyphs	Transliteration
	ḥtp-di-nsw ꜣsir nb ḏdw nṯr ꜥꜣ nb ꜣbḏw
	di=f prt-ḫrw t ḥnḳt kꜣ ꜣpd šs mnḫt
	ḫt nb(t) nfr(t) wꜥb(t) ꜥnḫt nṯr im
	n kꜣ n imꜣḫ(y) ky

An offering which the king gives (to) Osiris, lord of Djedu, great god, lord of Abydos, so that he may give a voice offering (in) bread, beer, ox, fowl, alabaster, linen, everything good and pure on which a god lives for the ka of the revered one Key

The most common form of the offering formula is composed of three parts, which can be divided according to the characteristic Egyptian expression found in each:

a.		*ḥtp-di-nsw*	an offering which the king gives
b.		*prt-ḫrw*	a voice offering
c.		*n kꜣ n*	for the ka of

We shall take you through each of these parts in turn, assembling here the material you need to be able to read the standard Osiris offering formula. If you return to this section when reading stelae such as BM EA 587 on p. 46 at the end of this chapter, you should find all the help you need. As you study the various stelae in this book, you will no doubt gain more and more familiarity with the various parts of the offering formula.

a. The offering to the god(s)

☥ ⬭ Λ   *ḥtp-di-nsw*   an offering which the king gives

The conventional grouping of this expression uses the following elements:

☥⬭	from	☥⬭	*nsw*	king
⬭	from	⬭	*ḥtp*	offering
Λ	from	Λ	*di*	give

(For the writing of the verb 'give', see Exercise 3.5.)

The expression *ḥtp-di-nsw* is often used to refer generally to the offering formula and its associated offering rites (and might less literally be translated as 'the offering rite'). The actual rendering of this stereotypical phrase is notoriously obscure and still exercises the minds of scholars. Whatever its original form, it is clear that by the Middle Kingdom the phrase had come to be treated as a fixed, compound expression. Here we have adopted a standard rendering which we encourage you to follow, rather than trying to work out its meaning from the individual signs.

The name, title and epithets of the god(s)
The name of the god then follows. The god most commonly named in the offering formula (as in the example above) is Osiris and we shall concentrate on him in this chapter. For the other common divine recipient of the offering formula, Anubis, see BM EA 1783 in Chapter 5, and for an example with a number of gods, see BM EA 584 in Chapter 8. The standard names and titles of Osiris are introduced separately in the notes on funerary deities at the end of this chapter.

b. The offerings are passed on to the deceased

The voice offering
This section of the offering formula centres around the following expression:

⬭   *prt-ḥrw*   a voice offering

The standard writing of *prt-ḥrw* contains the following elements:

⬭	from	⬭Λ	*prt*	a going forth
⎮	from	⬭	*ḥrw*	voice
⃝	from	⬭	*t*	bread
⬭	from	⬭	*ḥnḳt*	beer

The term *prt-ḥrw* is regularly written with the bread and beer signs, even when the voice offering itself is intended without any reference to the bread and beer. They are depicted whether bread and beer are mentioned separately in the subsequent inventory of offerings or not (in which case they may have been thought of as being included within the writing of *prt-ḥrw*).

By the Middle Kingdom *prt-ḥrw* had become a fixed expression used as a cover term for the offerings themselves (and might be loosely translated as 'the ritual offerings'). As a fixed expression, *prt-ḥrw* can even be written with a determinative for the whole phrase, such as ⊂⊃ 'loaf for offering':

$$\text{[glyphs]} \quad prt\text{-}ḥrw \quad \text{a voice offering}$$

The second part of the offering formula either starts off with *prt-ḥrw* immediately or marks the passing over of the offerings from the god by the use of:

$$\text{[glyphs]} \quad di{=}f \ prt\text{-}ḥrw \quad \text{so that he may give a voice offering}$$

di=f is again a form of the verb *rdi* 'to give' (see Exercise 3.5). Once again, at this stage we advise you to follow our suggested translation (see Chapter 8 for an explanation).

prt-ḥrw alone is typical of 11th-dynasty stelae. *di=f prt-ḥrw* is more typical from the mid-12th dynasty onwards (*prt-ḥrw* alone being rare by then). During the early part of the 12th dynasty a mixture of both usages is found.

The inventory of offerings:
The offerings are usually enumerated via a standard list of items, usually written with abbreviated writings (given here alongside fuller writings):

0 or [glyphs]	*t*	bread	[glyphs] or [glyphs]	*ḥnkt*	beer
[glyph] or [glyphs]	*kꜣ*	ox	[glyph] or [glyphs]	*ꜣpd*	fowl
[glyph] or [glyphs]	*šs*	alabaster	[glyphs] or [glyphs]	*mnḫt*	linen

Often the offerings are numbered with [glyph] *ḥꜣ* 'thousand' or [glyph] 'a thousand of/in'.

The voice offering from the stela of Tjeti:

$$\text{[glyphs]}$$

BM EA 614, Column 1:

prt-ḥrw ḥꜣ t ḥnkt ḥꜣ kꜣ ꜣpd ḥꜣ šs mnḫt
A voice offering (of) a thousand bread and beer, a thousand ox and fowl, a thousand alabaster and linen

(*prt-ḥrw* is here written with bread and beer signs but simply read *prt-ḥrw*; contrast with BM EA 558 on p. 36.)

Other offerings sometimes occur (particularly in later 12th- and 13th-dynasty stelae) and are usually more fully written out:

〔glyph〕	*mrḥt*	oil, unguent	〔glyph〕	*snṯr*	incense
〔glyph〕 or 〔glyph〕	*ḥtp* or *ḥtpt*	offerings	〔glyph〕	*df(ȝw)*	provisions

The inventory is wrapped up:
As well as listing a standard set of offerings, the offering formula also usually includes a more generic and all-embracing phrase:

〔glyph〕   *ḫt nb(t) nfr(t) wʿb(t)*   everything good and pure

You have already studied this expression in Exercise 2.4. It is often qualified by the following fixed expression:

〔glyph〕   *ʿnḫt nṯr im*   on which a god lives

Since this is a fixed expression, you should read and translate it as a whole for now, without worrying about its internal grammar (which will be explained in Chapter 7).

c. The recipient of the offering

The deceased recipient of the offering is introduced by one or both of the following phrases:

〔glyph〕   *n kȝ n*   for the ka of   〔glyph〕   *imȝḫ(w)*   the revered one

In the 11th dynasty and into the early 12th dynasty (after which it dies out), we usually find *imȝḫ(w)* on its own. The combined usage *n kȝ n imȝḫ(w)* begins in the early 12th dynasty and reaches its peak in the mid-12th dynasty. The use of *n kȝ n* on its own is rare in the early 12th dynasty, but becomes the most common form from the later 12th dynasty onwards.

Once you have reached this point, then you will find the name of the deceased, usually with a title, and ending with the common epithet:

〔glyph〕   *mȝʿ-ḫrw*   the justified

§27 The genitive
The genitive 'of' (as in 'the king of Egypt') occurs in two forms:

a. Direct genitive
The two nouns are put together without any linking word. This construction is only common between closely connected words or in fixed expressions:

𓀿𓉐	*m-r pr*	overseer of the estate		𓎟𓎛𓊖	*nb ꜣbḏw*	lord of Abydos (epithet of Osiris)
𓀿𓏏𓎟𓉐	*m-r ꜥẖnwty*	overseer of the chamber		𓎟𓊽𓂋	*nb ḏdw*	lord of Djedu (epithet of Osiris)

It also occurs in certain compound expressions, such as those compounded with *ib* 'heart':

    𓊨𓏤𓄣   *st-ib*   affection, intimacy (literally, situation of the heart)

st-ib occurs in a rather common epithet:

The stela of Ameny identifies his subordinate, Sahathor, with the epithet:

BM EA 162,   𓅡𓏤𓌳𓂝𓈖𓊨𓏤𓄣𓆑
Central column: *bꜣk=f mꜣꜥ n st-ib=f*
                His true servant of his affection

b. Indirect genitive

The two nouns are linked by forms of the 'genitival adjective' *n*. This behaves like an adjective and agrees with the preceding noun, taking the following forms:

SINGULAR		PLURAL	
MASCULINE	FEMININE	MASCULINE	FEMININE
〰 *n*	〰 *nt*	ⵔ *nw*	〰 *nt*

An example occurs in *bꜣk=f mꜣꜥ n st-ib=f* above. Another example occurs in the phrase:

    𓈖𓂓𓈖   *n kꜣ n*   for the ka of

〰 'of' is written in exactly the same way as the preposition 〰 *n* 'to', 'for'. However, in translating into English, one or other of these usually suggests itself (cf. 'for the ka of'). Also there is a tendency for *n* to be used for all numbers and genders, as in *ḥmt=f n st-ib=f* 'his wife of his affection' in Exercise 4.6.

Excursus: Egyptian funerary deities

Osiris

Osiris (*ꜣsir*) was a central figure in the funerary cults of the ancient Egyptians. As noted in Chapter 2, his name is written in an idiosyncratic manner and cannot easily be broken down sign by sign. Indeed there is still some dispute as to the exact reading – in this book we adopt the more recent suggestion to read *ꜣsir* rather than *wsir*, not least since this brings out the parallel with the writing of the name of Isis (for which see p. 42):

𓊨 or 𓊨𓁹   *ꜣsir*   Osiris   Written with E60-seat above A36-eye for reasons which are still obscure.

The writing of Osiris' name (and the number and nature of his epithets) altered at different periods of Egyptian history, as follows:

𓊨	*ꜣsir*	Osiris written without determinative (written with determinative in the 11th dynasty)	𓊨	Alternative writing from the late 12th dynasty

As a 'great god' (*nṯr ꜥꜣ*), the cult of Osiris was celebrated at many shrines, the most important of which are reflected in his titles 'lord of Djedu' and 'lord of Abydos', the writings of which you studied in Exercise 2.2. In BM EA 587 (see Exercise 3.8 below) they are written as follows:

𓎟𓊽𓊽⊗𓀭   *nb ḏdw*   lord of Djedu (written with graphic transposition, see §21)

𓊹𓉻   *nṯr ꜥꜣ*   great god   𓎟𓇋𓃀𓎿⊗   *nb ꜣbḏw*   lord of Abydos

These three together represent the classic Middle Kingdom combination of epithets, particularly common in the early 12th dynasty.

The writing of Djedu itself changes over time (as well as sometimes displaying graphic transposition):

𓊽𓂝𓊽	11th – mid-12th dynasty	𓊽𓂝𓊽⊗ or 𓂝𓊽⊗	11th – early 12th dynasty	𓊽𓊽𓊽⊗	late 12th dynasty onward

The pre-eminence of Osiris is reflected in his other name, Khentyimentu (*ḫnty-imntw*), 'the one who is foremost of the westerners' (i.e. the dead gathered in the realm of the setting sun); the name evokes his subjects (the dead spirits) arrayed before his throne:

𓏃𓏏𓋀𓁹   *ḫnty-imntw*   Khentyimentu

As will become clear from a number of the stelae which you will study in this book, the name Khentyimentu is often included in the offering formula amongst the epithets of Osiris (again typical of the early 12th dynasty).

In mythology, Osiris had been a living king at the beginning of history, but was murdered and dismembered by his ambitious brother, Seth. Osiris' remains were magically restored by Isis (*ꜣst*) – his sister – who was then able to conceive his child, Horus; Horus grew up to defeat Seth and inherit his father's throne in legitimate fashion. Osiris is represented as a deceased king,

mummiform but with royal regalia, and a green or black complexion allud-
ing to the fertility of the Nile floodplain.

    ⟨glyph⟩ or ⟨glyph⟩   *ꜣst*   Isis   ⟨glyph⟩   *ḥr*   Horus

The passion of Osiris is also reflected in the name Wenennefer (*wnn-nfr*),
which means 'the one who continues to be perfect' and hints at his mysterious *post mortem* potency:

    ⟨glyph⟩   *wnn-nfr*   Wenennefer

Wepwawet and Anubis

Funerary stelae from Abydos and elsewhere often invoke Wepwawet and
Anubis alongside Osiris. Represented as a dog or jackal, Wepwawet (*wp-
wꜣwt*) was an ancient god of Abydos and an active participant in the cult of
Osiris: the annual passion-play at Abydos began with the procession of Wepwawet 'to protect his father', Osiris. More generally, Wepwawet was
associated with cemeteries and funerals, as reflected in his title 'lord of the
sacred land' (*nb tꜣ ḏsr*), where 'sacred land' means the cemetery. Even the
name Wepwawet (literally, 'the one who opens the ways', see p. 96) recalls
the untrodden paths over the desert along which he guided the souls of the
newly deceased to the kingdom of Osiris.

    The other major funerary deity was Anubis, whose iconography is
close to that of Wepwawet; he also appears in canine form and bears the title
'lord of the sacred land'; his other titles are more obscure. Nevertheless, the
funerary gods have distinct roles, apparent in the mythology of the funeral:
Anubis embalmed the body of the deceased and conducted the burial cere-
monies; Wepwawet led the deceased from this world to the next; and Osiris,
king of the dead, represented arrival and rejuvenation in the next life.

Anubis

The name and standard epithets of Anubis:

⟨glyph⟩   *inpw*   Anubis   ⟨glyph⟩   *tp(y) ḏw=f*   upon his mountain

⟨glyph⟩   *im(y)-wt*   the one in the *wt*   ⟨glyph⟩   *nb tꜣ ḏsr*   lord of the sacred land

Wepwawet

Wepwawet shares a major epithet with Anubis:

⟨glyph⟩   *wp-wꜣwt*   Wepwawet   ⟨glyph⟩   *nb tꜣ ḏsr*   lord of the sacred land

Exercises

3.1 Signs and words

a. 2-consonant and 3-consonant signs

𓄿	*ꜣb* or *mr*	𓃹 *wn*	𓃀 *bḥ* or *ḥw*	𓉔 *ḥn*
𓂝 *wꜥ*	𓅨 *wr*	𓂧 *nw* or *in*	𓎛 *ḫnt*

As you will see below, the name of the god Khentyimentu displays the *tw*-bird (B5 long-legged buzzard), a sign which reads *tw* or *tyw* (in this book we shall go for the simpler reading *tw*), but looks similar to the *ꜣ*-bird (B3 Egyptian vulture). The *tw*-bird has a more rounded head, but often the two birds are very similar in writing (sometimes we add a tick to the *tw*-bird to distinguish it). Fortunately the *tw*-bird has a very restricted usage:

𓅮 or 𓅮 *tw*   𓅐 *ꜣ*

b. Ideograms

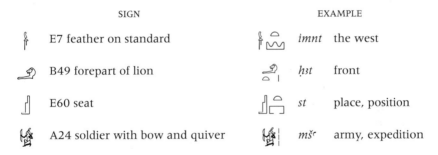

	SIGN		EXAMPLE	
𓆂	E7 feather on standard	𓋀	*imnt*	the west
𓄂	B49 forepart of lion	𓄂	*ḥꜣt*	front
𓊨	E60 seat	𓊨	*st*	place, position
𓀎	A24 soldier with bow and quiver	𓀎	*mšꜥ*	army, expedition

Notice that the sign 𓊨 has appeared in two different words which should not be confused:

𓊨 or 𓊨𓀭 *ꜣsir* Osiris   𓊨 *st* place, position

3.2 Words

Transliterate the following words (one uses a sign introduced in an earlier chapter):

𓅨 .... great   𓇋𓏠𓈖𓇌𓇌 .... Ameny (name)

3.3 Gods' names

You have already been introduced to two forms of Osiris: Khentyimentu and Wenennefer. These are written as follows. Transliterate:

𓎛𓆂𓅮𓀭 .... Khentyimentu   𓃹𓈖𓈖𓆑𓂋𓀭 .... Wenennefer

3.4 *Titles*

In the text, the following two titles were introduced. Here they are written in a slightly different way. Transliterate them, using the sign-tables above:

overseer of
the chamber ....

sole
.... companion

3.5 *Common verbs*

Some common verbs are written with otherwise uncommon signs and with some idiosyncracies of their own. It will be useful for you to be familiar with these when reading Chapter 4 (where the presence of (*i*) in brackets will also be explained):

in(i) 'bring', written with a combination of ○ D33 pot and A57 walking legs, often with sound complement ﹏ *n*

ir(i) 'make', 'do', 'act' – written with the 2-consonant sign ⌖ *ir*

mꜣꜣ *mꜣꜣ* 'see', 'look at' – written with ⌖ determinative placed under *mꜣ*. Some forms of this verb are written with only one *ꜣ* – transliterated *mꜣ*

rdi 'give', 'place' – A41 arm giving loaf, or E61 conical loaf. Without *r* as or, transliterated *di*. From the hieratic, also written with arm as *rdi* or *di*

3.6 *The offering formula from BM EA 162*

BM EA 162
(carved limestone; w. 75cm)

The offering formula is usually written in a telegram-like style with very abbreviated writings and certain prepositions omitted. The top portion of the stela of Ameny (BM EA 162), however, rather unusually provides us with a more fully written out version of certain sections of the offering formula.

Transliterate and translate, using the template provided in the text (§26 above), and study the individual writings of the various component parts of the formula. You should also make use of the vocabulary introduced in the other exercises above.

VOCABULARY

⌢	*ir-n*	born of		⌇	*=f*	he, his (pronoun)
🦅⌢𓀀𓅃	*m-r mšꜥ wr*	general-in-chief		⊜	*ḫr*	before, in front of
◿𓂋𓅃	*ḳbw*	Qebu (name)				

Notes:

i *ir-n* means 'whom such-and-such a person made' but this is not a satisfactory idiom in English.

ii *m-r mšꜥ wr* means literally 'great overseer of the army'.

iii In line 1, the damaged hieroglyphs are part of the standard epithets of Osiris: *ḫnty-imntw* (with an extra *tw*-bird), *nṯr ꜥꜣ, nb ꜣbḏw* (see p. 41).

3.7 Offering table scene

Meir I, pl. 9

In scenes, the offerings are often shown placed on a table before the deceased. Transliterate and translate the hieroglyphs below the offering table scene from the tomb of Senbi (consult the section on the offering formula if necessary).

VOCABULARY

ḥȝty-ꜥ	governor, mayor		ḫȝ(w)	thousands

The laden offering table constituting the 'funerary meal' for the deceased is referred to as:

or   dbḥt-ḥtp   the required offerings

3.8 Study exercise: BM EA 587

BM EA 587
(carved and painted limestone; H. 56cm)

It is now time for you to study your first stela – BM EA 587, the funerary monument of the overseer of the chamber Amenemhet. Transliterate and translate the hieroglyphs written within the registers (and not those accompanying the vases at the top left, written without registers). You should consult the sections on the offering formula in the text (§26) where necessary. You may also find it useful to read through the notes on Osiris given on pp. 40–42.

VOCABULARY

[hieroglyphs]	*m-r* *ꜥḥnw(ty)*	overseer of the chamber	[hieroglyphs]	*imn-m-ḥꜣt*	Amenemhet

(See p. 102 for some remarks on the title *m-r ꜥḥnwty*.)

Notice that the inscription has been carefully laid out: the *ḥtp-di-nsw* formula takes up the first line; the *prt-ḥrw* formula the second line and the epithets, name and titles of the stela owner the third line.

3.9 Study exercise: BM EA 585
BM EA 585, shown on the next page, has another standard offering formula, this time written from right to left.

a. Translation
Transliterate and translate, using the notes and vocabulary below.

Notice how the names of Sarenenutet and his mother Bameket are written to fit the space available. The scenes and figures are in raised relief and the inscriptions in sunk relief. The element *-mkt* in the mother's name is written in the scene area and in raised relief.

VOCABULARY

[hieroglyphs]	*bꜣ-mkt*	Bameket	[hieroglyphs]	*ms-n*	born of
[hieroglyphs]	*nṯrw*	gods	[hieroglyphs]	*ḥsb šnwty*	counter of the double granaries
[hieroglyphs]	*dd ḥtp-nṯr*	offering-giver	[hieroglyphs]	*sꜣ-rnnwtt*	Sarenenutet

b. Epigraphy
Compare this stela with BM EA 587:
  i Identify the differences in the shape and arrangement of particular hieroglyphs (you may also wish to consider the figures and the offering tables).
 ii Identify the differences in the phraseology of the offering formula.

BM EA 585
(carved limestone; H. 52cm)

Chapter 4

Scenes and captions

The first part of this book was dedicated primarily to building up your knowledge of the hieroglyphic signs needed to equip you for the twin goals of reading the names of the kings and the offering formula. In this part of the book we will move on to broaden your knowledge of the ancient Egyptian language and how it works, equipping you to read a wider range of Middle Kingdom stelae in the British Museum and elsewhere, and also supplying you with a firm foundation for moving on to study the wealth of surviving ancient Egyptian writings.

§28 Captions: the infinitive

Verbs typically label actions or events such as 'do', or 'kick', though some verbs label states or conditions such as 'remain'. A major topic to be dealt with in reading hieroglyphs is how to get the right translation of verbs according to whether they refer to actions in the past, present or future. Over the next few chapters we will equip you to bring this degree of accuracy to your translations.

A good place to start is with scenes and captions. Scenes are often accompanied by captions which very conveniently label the action:

spt smḥ   Binding a skiff (Meir II, pl. 4)

(In captions, words are often written without determinatives, since the image itself pictures the meaning.)

In English the *-ing* form of the verb translates rather well here, whereas using the simple English past 'bound a skiff' seems a little incomplete and unsatisfactory. Exactly the same is true in Egyptian. In such captions, Egyptian uses a particular form of the verb which, as you will see in the next chapter, differs markedly from the form for expressing the past. In Egyptian the equivalent of the *-ing* form in this usage is termed the *infinitive* (see §31 below for its forms).

Before we progress further, there is one general comment we would like to make. The terms for the various Egyptian verb-forms are now rather traditional; they are not always very clear in their meaning, nor do they always agree with the use of the same term in describing the grammar of English. So the term 'infinitive' and its meaning is not really important – it will, however, serve as a convenient label by which we can readily refer to the verb-form.

When the actor is mentioned in an Egyptian caption, this is usually introduced by ⟨ ⁓⁓⁓ *in* 'by':

Before the figure of the owner is a lengthy adoration caption, the bare bones of which are:

BM EA 567:   *sn tꜣ n ḫnty-imntw m prt ꜥꜣt ... in m-r šnꜥ(w) imn-m-ḥꜣt*
Kissing the ground to Khentyimentu in the great procession ... by the overseer of the provisioning areas Amenemhet

For the vocabulary, see the next section and the excursus on titles, p. 103.

§29 Adoration

The owner of a stela often expressed a wish to participate in certain important festivals beyond death, particularly the Osiris Mysteries (for which see pp. 54–56). He either wished to participate in them directly – through seeing (*mꜣꜣ*), adoring (*dwꜣ*), kissing the ground (*sn tꜣ*), or giving praise (*dit iꜣw*) to the god – or through having offerings made to him at such times. For example:

The vertical columns of stela BM EA 580 comprise a hymn to Osiris which begins:

BM EA 580,
Lines 1-2:   *dit iꜣw n ꜣsir sn tꜣ n wp-wꜣwt*
Giving praise to Osiris, kissing the ground to Wepwawet

§30 Verb classes and the infinitive

So how does this all work? The first and most basic point is that when deciding on the exact translation to be adopted (for example, should we

translate 'kissing' in the example above as opposed to 'kissed' or 'will kiss'?),
two points should be borne in mind:

i   what help does the writing of the verb give us? (the question of *form*)

ii how does the verb fit in the context of the inscription? (the question of *function*)

As you will see, since hieroglyphs only write consonants and not vowels, the hieroglyphic writing alone will not always direct us to the exact form. However, once we take into account how the verb seems to be being used in the inscription, then we can usually get good sense out of it. The first 'tool of the trade' that we need to introduce you to is the topic of verb classes. All the verbs in ancient Egyptian can be gathered into a small number of groups, which, when considered as a whole (or *paradigm*), usually allow us to see each form somewhat more clearly. The following are the standard verb classes with a convenient example for each class:

VERB CLASS		EXAMPLE AND DESCRIPTION		
STRONG VERBS	e.g.	*sḏm*	to hear	stem does not usually show any alteration
DOUBLING VERBS	e.g.	*m33*	to see	stem ends in a double consonant
WEAK VERBS	e.g.	*mr(i)*	to love	stem ends with a 'weak' consonant, usually *-i*
EXTRA WEAK VERBS	e.g.	*rd(i)*	to give	chiefly verbs with two or three weak consonants

Notes

i   With weak verbs, the final *-i* is usually omitted in writing and therefore in transliteration. For practical reasons, however, we will transliterate the extra weak verb 'to give' as *rdi* or *di*.

ii Extra weak verbs behave like ordinary weak verbs, but sometimes show additional features.

The stem of a strong verb is not usually that helpful since it rarely shows any differences. As you will see below, the infinitive of strong verbs gives us little written clue. Doubling verbs have a root which ends with the same consonant repeated twice. In writing, some forms of these verbs show only one of these consonants (e.g. *m3*) and in other forms show two (e.g. *m33*) and this can help in distinguishing certain forms. Weak and extra weak verbs, whose roots end in a 'weak consonant' (*-i* or *-w*), are the most interesting because they show a wider range of variation in different verb-forms, which can be most useful in spotting a particular form (we shall see that weak verb infinitives are rather more easy to spot than strong verb infinitives).

One important point to note about weak verbs is that the *-i* and *-w* with which their root or dictionary forms end do not usually appear in writing and so need not be transliterated. However, so that you can see readily whether a verb is a weak verb or not, the *-i* or *-w* of weak verbs will be added in brackets (as in the table above) in the vocabularies in this book.

§31   The forms of the infinitive

So let's turn to the infinitive and see how all this works out. The infinitive in Egyptian has the following form:

		INFINITIVE	
STRONG VERBS - no change		*sḏm*	hearing
DOUBLING VERBS - doubling		*m33*	seeing
WEAK VERBS - end in *-t*		*mrt*	loving
EXTRA WEAK VERBS - end in *-t*	or	*rdit* or *dit*	giving/placing (*r* optional in both writings, see p. 44)

Here are some examples to illustrate this:

STRONG VERBS   Meir I, pl. 2:

ʿmʿ3 r 3pd(w)
Throwing at the birds

DOUBLING VERBS   Meir I, pl. 9:

m33 iw3w
Seeing the cattle

WEAK VERBS   Meir II, pl. 4:

spt smḥ
Binding a skiff

EXTRA WEAK VERBS   BM EA 580, 1:

dit i3w n 3sir
Giving praise to Osiris

The most noticeable feature of the table is that the form of the infinitive of weak verbs ends in a *-t*. Consider again the scene and caption with which we introduced this chapter (repeated on p. 53).

If you look at the vocabulary at the end of the book, you will find the following word listed:

sp(i)   bind (together)

(𓎛 D11 coil of rope is a common determinative for ropes, cords and actions performed with them.)

𓊪𓂝𓏏𓊃 *spt smḥ*   Binding a skiff

Just like English dictionaries, dictionaries and word-lists of ancient Egyptian just give you a standard citation form (the *root*), here *sp(i)* 'bind (together)', and do not tell whether you need 'binding', 'bound' or whatever in your actual translation. All the citation form tells us is that *sp(i)* is a **weak verb**. But if we look at the actual example we find the following form, showing an extra *t*:

𓊪𓂝𓏏   *spt*   binding

and also, of course, it is being used in a caption. Together this information allows us to decide that *spt* is an example of the Egyptian infinitive and can be translated well into English as 'bind-**ing**'.

We advise you at this stage to follow our example here in adhering to a small number of suggested *translation schemes* for the various forms we will introduce you to, since this will help you to get good sense out of the hieroglyphic inscriptions you will read in this book. At first, it is better to refrain from trying to be more imaginative or to 'guestimate' the meaning. So our first translation scheme is for the infinitive (simply substitute the necessary verb for 'do'):

infinitive translation scheme   **doing** or **to do**

In the examples in this chapter 'doing' will be the right choice, but on other occasions 'to do' will fit better. If the range of meaning seems a bit loose, compare the English '**To study** hieroglyphs is interesting' with '**Studying** hieroglyphs is interesting' where the English 'to do' and 'doing' forms have a similar usage.

Now, of course, infinitives of strong and doubling verbs do not offer us much help in their writing. But the context and sometimes other parallel examples can help out. As an example, we can consider again the fishing and fowling scene from the tomb of Senbi which you studied in edited form in Chapter 1 and which you can study in its original, complete form as Exercise 4.6. The two edited labels were:

a. Scene of spearing fish:

Meir I, pl. 2:

stt rm(w) in snbi mꜣꜥ-ḫrw
Spearing fish by Senbi, the justified

b. Scene of throwing the throw-stick at the birds:

Meir I, pl. 2:

ꜥmꜣꜣ r ꜣpd(w) in snbi mꜣꜥ-ḫrw
Throwing at the birds by Senbi, the justified

st(i) 'spear' is a weak verb, hence the infinitive *stt* 'spearing'. *ꜥmꜣꜣ*, however, is a strong verb and does not provide a particularly helpful writing. Yet the context of the caption and the parallel with the other caption showing us *stt* 'spearing' urge us to consider the infinitive and the translation 'throw**ing**'. Notice also how using the suggested translation scheme helps us to draw together a decent English translation of the whole: 'throwing at the birds by Senbi the justified', whereas reasonable alternatives such as 'throws at the birds' do not: 'throws at the birds by Senbi the justified' is not particularly good English.

Excursus: The cult of Osiris at Abydos

The heart of the cult of Osiris at Abydos was the annual festival at which his cult-statue was brought, in a ritual boat carried aloft by priests, in procession from his temple to his supposed tomb at Umm el-Qaꜥab ('mother of pots'). The festival procession had two fundamental components – a public section during which the divine image passed through the cemetery abutting the temple's western side, and a private section out in the desert where the secret rites concerning the mysteries and passion of Osiris were performed. During the Middle Kingdom at Abydos, members of the élite dedicated stelae, or erected offering chapels as cenotaphs, hoping to ensure their continued participation in the festival after their own death. The cemetery at Abydos was therefore a veritable city of the dead with a wealth of monuments, and, as you will see, Abydene stelae form an important body of the Middle Kingdom monuments studied in this book.

Here we shall concentrate on the route of the festival. In Exercise 6.5, you will study one of the principal surviving ancient sources for the festival procession itself. The exact location and scope of the various Egyptian place names used are still a matter for debate. However, the map below gives a plausible version.

The starting point of the festival procession was the Osiris Temple (   ), housing the statue of the god. As you will see for yourself in Exercise 6.5, there were actually two outward processions – the 'procession of Wepwawet' (   ) and then the 'great procession' of Osiris (   ). Stelae were concentrated near the western entrance to the temple, in an area of high ground known as the 'terrace of the great god' (   ), so that the deceased could look upon the emergence and return of the gods (hence the references to 'kissing the ground' and 'giving praise' as the images of the gods pass by – the cult images of the gods are often referred to as their   *nfrw* 'splendour'). The procession crossed the terrace before descending into a wadi (the sacred land,   ). The god then proceeded out into the desert on the God's boat-journey (   ) to Poker (   ) where the divine mysteries and rites were performed. Abydos had a long history as one of the most sacred sites in the country since it was at Umm el-Qaʿab that the earliest kings were buried. By the 12th

Dynasty, the tomb of the 1st-dynasty king Djer was believed to be that of Osiris himself.

VOCABULARY

	prt	procession		*rwd*	terrace
	prt ꜥꜣt	the great procession		*ḥwt-nṯr*	temple
	prt wp-wꜣwt	the procession of Wepwawet		*tꜣ ḏsr*	sacred land
	pḳr	Poker		*ḏꜣt nṯr*	god's boat-journey

Exercises

4.1 Signs

a. Sound signs:

in   *sn*   *wḥm*

ḥm   *m(w)t*   *dwꜣ*

b. Determinatives:

SIGN   EXAMPLE

F6 basin combined with canopy   or   *ḥb*   festival

A20 man with outstretched arms   or   *iꜣ(w)*   praise, adoration

Both of these determinatives are used widely, for various festivals and for words to do with praise and supplication. Note, however, that when used on their own, they are abbreviated writings of the two specific words given.

4.2 Words

Transliterate the following words:

. . . .   sister   . . . .   wife

. . . .   adore, praise   . . . .   kiss

. . . .   brother   . . . .   repeat

4.3 Translation

Transliterate and translate the two captions on the following page:

Meir II, pl. 4

The bull is also labelled separately between the two figures at the top.

Meir I, pl. 11

VOCABULARY (NORMALISED WRITINGS)

	wp(i)	separate, open		or	*ng3w*	long-horned bull
	sph	lassoo			*k3*	bull

4.4 Translation

Transliterate and translate the following sections from the top of BM EA 101, the stela of Nebipusenwosret, dating from the reign of Amenemhet III (shown on the next page – ignore the sections in grey). You may wish to read the notes on the cult of Osiris at Abydos on pp. 54–56 for useful background information.

The following notes will help you in translating the central section:

Notes

i   The eye emblem in the centre can be read as a verb 'to see'. It is thought to read *ptr* 'to see, view', rather than *m33*. The form is the infinitive.

ii   See §§17–18 on the king's name and epithets (the epithets are divided
     into two columns mirroring the general division into a section on Osiris
     on the left and one on Wepwawet on the right). *mry* is used in the epi-
     thet 'beloved of the god X'. The name of the god (and his titles) are
     written first for reasons of prestige (as noted in §22 above).

BM EA 101
(carved and painted limestone; w. 66cm)

The deceased king Senwosret III forms the central focus of the scene. As
recorded in 'the middle section of the stela, Nebipusenwosret had this stela
sent to Abydos in the care of the elder lector-priest Ibi who had come, as part
of the priesthood of the temple of Abydos, to the residence of the then reigning king Amenemhet III.

VOCABULARY

	prt	procession		*ptr nfrw*	viewing the splendour
	=f	his		*m*	in, during
	nb(=i)-pw-snwsrt	Nebipu-senwosret		*nfr*	perfect, wonderful
	nfrw	perfection, beauty, wonder, splendour		*ḥb(w)*	festivals
	dwȝ	adore, praise		*ḏt r nḥḥ*	enduringly and repeatedly

Grammar

As noted in §10, adjectives follow and agree with their nouns. Exercise 4.4
provides examples of feminine and plural agreement (cf. §§8 and 15 above):

	prt=f nfrt	his wonderful procession
	prt ꜥзt	the great procession
	ḥb(w)=f nfrw	his wonderful festivals

4.5 Translation

Transliterate and translate the following sections on the next page from BM EA 581, one of the three stelae of the overseer of the chamber Intef son of Senet in the British Museum. These stelae are extremely elaborate in their wording, so we will only consider two sections. Ignore the parts in grey.

BM EA 581
(carved limestone; w. 36cm)

VOCABULARY

	intf	Intef		*ir-n*	born of
	mз3	see, look at		*nfrw*	splendour, wonder
	sn	kiss		*snt*	Senet
	tз	land, ground			

Writings

The extracts from BM EA 581 show two variant writings worth noting:

and	*ḫnty-imntw*	Khentyimentu	The first sign has two variants, with three or four pots (E38, E39)
and	*m-r ꜥḫnwty*	overseer of the chamber	*ḥ* and *ḫ* are similar sounds and can occur in variant writings

4.6 Study exercise: Fishing and fowling scene from the tomb of Senbi at Meir

You are now in a position to transliterate and translate the original version of the fishing and fowling scene from the tomb of Senbi shown on page 61.

VOCABULARY

	ꜣpd(w)	fowl, birds		*nb, nbt*	lord (masc.) lady (fem.)
	ib	heart		*r*	at, towards
	imꜣḫ	reverence		*rm(w)*	fish
	imꜣḫy	the revered		*ḥꜣty-ꜥ*	governor
	imntt	western		*ḥmt*	wife
	in	by		*ḥr*	before
	ꜣsir	Osiris		*ḥtmty-bity*	seal-bearer of the king
	ꜥmꜣ	throw		*smyt*	desert
	=f	his		*smr-wꜥt(y)*	sole companion
or	*mꜣꜥ-ḫrw*	justified		*snbi*	Senbi
	m-r ḥm-nṯr	overseer of priests		*st-ib*	affection, intimacy
	mrs	Meres		*st(i)*	spear

Notes

i Fishing scene: ancient correction at end of line, read: [hieroglyphs].

ii Fowling scene: end of first line, read [hieroglyphs]. Above wife, read ~~~~ *n* 'of' above [hieroglyph].

(Meir I, pl. 2)

4.7 Study exercise: The coffin of Nakhtankh (BM EA 35285)

Although in this book we concentrate on stelae in the British Museum, the material that you are working through also puts you in a position to study inscriptions on other kinds of museum objects, particularly where they include the offering formula. In this exercise you will study the inscriptions on the outside of a Middle Kingdom coffin (BM EA 35285, the coffin of Nakhtankh).

We shall concentrate on the two exterior sides of the coffin, omitting the inscriptions on the head and foot ends. The inscriptions are aligned on the coffin as follows:

The body was laid on its left side, facing towards the east, in order to be able to look out through the eyes on the eastern side towards the newly rejuvenated sun at sunrise. Hence the inscriptions run from the head at the northern end towards the feet at the southern end. This represents the typical arrangement of a Middle Kingdom rectangular coffin. On the eastern side (the side with the eyes looking out towards the sunrise), the main inscription is an offering formula to Osiris. On the western side is an offering formula to Anubis. At the corners, the inscriptions invoke the four sons of Horus, protective deities for the body of the deceased (with the classic Middle Kingdom arrangement of Imseti and Duamutef on the east side and Hapy and Qebehsenuef on the west). The central columns invoke deities closely linked to Osiris: Shu and Geb on the east side and their female consorts Tefnet and Nut on the west.

The eastern side

The eastern side of the coffin is shown on the next page. Transliterate and translate with the help of the vocabulary and notes below:

BM EA 35285 (eastern side)
(painted wood; L. 212cm)

Notes

i *imȝḫ(y) ḥr* displays haplography (i.e., where the last sign in one word and the first in the next are the same and the sign is written only once).

ii *mȝꜥ-ḫrw* is (a) written occasionally with the papyrus-roll and (b) omitted in the northernmost column.

iii the *gb*-goose (B8) is different from the *sȝ*-duck (B7).

VOCABULARY

	nḫt-ꜥnḫ	Nakhtankh
	ḫnt(y)-imntw	Khentyimentu

THE FOUR SONS OF HORUS			OTHER DEITIES		
	imsti	Imseti		*šw*	Shu
	dwȝ-mwt=f	Duamutef		*gb*	Geb
	ḥpy	Hapy		*tfnt*	Tefnet
	ḳbḥ-snw=f	Qebehsenuef		*nwt*	Nut

The western side

The principal inscription on the western side of the coffin is an offering formula to Anubis. Whereas the Osiris offering formula concerns the offerings to sustain the ka of the deceased, the Anubis offering formula concerns the burial itself.

Transliterate and translate with the help of the following notes:

BM EA 35285 (western side)

Notes

i   The standard organization of the Anubis offering formula is: *ḥtp-di-nsw* followed by Anubis with his epithets and then *ḳrst nfrt* without being introduced by *di=f*. You may wish to introduce your translation of *ḳrst nfrt* with a dash or colon after the *ḥtp-di-nsw* section.

ii Read *is=f nfr n ḥrt-nṯr* with the indirect genitive (see §27 above). *is=f* means 'his tomb'; for *=f* see §33.

iii Anubis is invoked with his standard epithets (see p. 42) and a further epithet:

   ḫnty sḥ-nṯr   the one before the divine booth

VOCABULARY

	is	tomb		*nfr*	good, perfect, wonderful
	ḥrt-nṯr	cemetery, necropolis		*ḳrst*	burial

Chapter 5

Description

In the next two chapters, we will introduce you to the past tense, concentrating on inscriptions in which the deceased reflects back upon, and describes, his official life. We will also introduce you to the ancient Egyptian pronouns.

§32 Introduction: description

In a typical type of funerary inscription – which we can term *self-presentation* – the owner presents himself (rarely, herself) according to the ethical values of Middle Kingdom élite society and in terms of success and achievement, particularly in royal service. In order to *describe* the *activities* which the official participated in, the *tasks* he accomplished, and his *ethical behaviour*, the past tense is generally used.

The official Intef son of Senet proclaims his ethical behaviour:

BM EA 562,
Line 10:

iw ḳrs.n=i i3(w)
I buried the old

This construction comprises the past form of the verb (ḳrs + ‿‿‿ *.n*; cf. English 'bury' + '-ed' – see §33 below) *followed* by the subject ('I') and other elements; the sentence begins with an auxiliary *iw* which is not translated into English (see §34 below).

§33 The past: *sḏm.n(=f)*

The past form is termed the *sḏm.n(=f)* (pronounced 'sedjemenef') 'he heard', using the verb *sḏm* 'to hear' in the 'he' form ('he heard') as the standard example. In this form, an affix ‿‿‿ *.n* '-ed', is added to the verb-stem (written after the determinative). As a standard convention, in trans-literation the *.n* is usually separated from the stem of the verb by a dot – this just makes it easier to spot. The forms of the *sḏm.n(=f)* for the verb classes (§30 above) are:

$$s\underline{d}m.n(=f)$$

STRONG VERBS		*sḏm.n=f*	he heard
DOUBLING VERBS		*mȝ.n=f* no doubling	he saw
WEAK VERBS		*mr.n=f*	he loved
EXTRA WEAK VERBS		*(r)di.n=f* *r* optional	he gave

When there is a pronoun subject (e.g. 'I heard', 'he heard'), the *suffix pronouns* are used (see §36 below); the pronouns for 'I' and 'he' are given here (compare with the example above):

SUFFIX PRONOUNS				$s\underline{d}m.n(=f)$		
I		*=i*			*sḏm.n=i*	I heard
He/It		*=f*			*sḏm.n=f*	he heard

The suffix pronouns (see the reference tables on p. 148 for a full list) attach to the verb; this is indicated in transliteration by the symbol '='. Once again this has the practical value of making the suffix pronouns easy to spot in transliteration: *sḏm.n=f* is much easier to read (*sḏm* 'hear' + .*n* '-d' + =*f* 'he') than *sḏmnf*.

   With an ordinary noun subject (e.g. 'the man heard'), the noun follows the verb, but does not fix onto it (hence there is no '=' in transliteration):

Hekaib records an inspection of his property by the ruler:

BM EA 167,
Line 10:

iw ip.n ḥkȝ iwȝ(w)(=i)
The ruler inspected my cattle

(For the omission of =*i* in *iwȝ(w)=i* 'my cattle', see §35 below; see p. 73 for vocabulary.)

§34 Auxiliaries

The *sḏm.n(=f)* is usually preceded by an auxiliary such as ⟨𓇋𓅱⟩ *iw*. In stela inscriptions *iw sḏm.n(=f)* often translates well as a simple past ('someone did something'):

Inhuretnakht extols his proper conduct as a responsible official:

BM EA 1783,
Line 4:

iw rdi.n(=i) t n ḥkr ḥbsw n ḥȝy
I gave bread to the hungry and clothes to the naked

(There is no word for 'and' in Egyptian; for vocabulary, see Exercise 5.4.)

There is no simple English equivalent for *iw* and so it is left untranslated. It invokes a sense of involvement in the assessment or presentation of what is said/written. In self-presentation inscriptions, *iw sḏm.n(=f)* gives a sense of looking back over one's life. In other contexts the perfect ('someone has done something') also suits, particularly in recorded speech.

§35 Omission of the first person suffix pronoun

The first person suffix pronoun ('I-me-my') is sometimes omitted in writing, particularly in texts where a figure of the person is present (e.g. stelae and tomb inscriptions) or strongly implied (e.g. where the text is all about that person):

Another of Inhuretnakht's stated ethical acts:

BM EA 1783,
Lines 4-5:

iw ḏȝ.n(=i) iww <m> mḫnt(=i) ḏs(=i)
I ferried the boatless in my own ferry

Note:

i *iww* 'the boatless' is written with a doubling of the 2-consonant sign B32.

ii Repeated consonants are sometimes omitted: here only one *m* is written in *m mḫnt(=i)* 'in my ferry'.

iii *ḏs* is used for the emphatic reflexive '(my/him)self' or 'own'.

§36 Suffix pronouns

Although, as we shall see, there are different sets of pronouns in Egyptian with different usages, they do not correspond to the difference between 'I-me-my' or 'he-him-his' in English. The Egyptian pronouns translate by whatever happens to be the most appropriate English form of pronoun. The suffix pronouns are used:

a. As the subjects of verbs ('I', 'he')

The official Intef son of Senet proclaims his ethical behaviour:

BM EA 562,
Line 10:

iw ḳrs.n=i iȝ(w)
I buried the old

b. As the possessor of a noun ('my', 'his')

The top part of BM EA 101 behind the figure of Nebipusenwosret (see p. 58):

BM EA 101:

dwꜣ ꜣsir m ḥb(w)=f nfrw ḏt r nḥḥ
Adoring Osiris in **his** wonderful festivals enduringly and repeatedly

c.   As the object after a preposition ('me', 'him')

From the Abydos formula on BM EA 162:

BM EA 162,
Line 5:

ḏd.t(w)=f n=f iw m ḥtp in wrw n ꜣbḏw
May 'Welcome in peace' be said for **him** by the great of Abydos

(For the meaning of ḏd.t(w)=f, see p. 115.)
For the full list of suffix pronouns, see Reference table, p. 148.

§37 The past relative form: *sḏmt.n(=f)*

The following paragraph discusses a more advanced point which some of you may wish to work through at this stage in order to gain the maximum understanding of the inscriptions read as study exercises to this chapter. Others may consider these points a little abstruse at this stage and may prefer to return to this paragraph later on.

As well as being *described* ('someone did something'), events can also be *characterised* (treated as a 'thing which someone did': 'what/which someone did'). Egyptian has a special way of characterising an event – by using the *relative forms* – which is quite different from English and is often seen as one of the more difficult aspects of ancient Egyptian. However, the use of the relative forms is extremely common and will crop up in a number of examples, and so we will attempt to open up this area of Egyptian for you by the use of our notion of a translation scheme. The difference between description and characterisation can be seen in the following example:

The self-presentation of Inhuretnakht ends:

BM EA 1783,
Line 5:

iw ir.n(=i) kꜣw 100 m irt.n(=i) ḏs(=i)
I assembled 100 bulls through what I did myself

Notes
   i ꜥ is the number 100.
  ii *m* here has the meaning 'through' or 'by the means of'.
 iii *ir(i)* 'to do' has a wide range of idiomatic meanings.
  iv =*i* is omitted (see §35 above).

In Egyptian, the described event 'I assembled 100 bulls' is expressed by using the *sḏm.n(=f)* form *ir.n(=i)*. However, the characterised event 'what I did myself' is expressed by using another verb-form – *the past relative form: irt.n(=i)*. In this usage, there is no separate word for 'what' or 'which', rather the verb-form shows a *-t* in its writing, so *irt.n(=i)* in itself means 'what I did' without needing extra words. Notice that missing out a word such as 'what' in translation leaves the sentence with poor sense: 'I assembled a hundred bulls through I did myself'. You will often find this to be the case: the relative forms (and their cousins, the participles introduced in Chapter 7) scream out for the inclusion of an English word such as 'what' or 'which' in translation. The same stela provides another similar example:

Between the figures of Inhuretnakht and Hui, the following dedication label about the stela appears:

BM EA 1783:

irt.n -n=f sꜣ=f smsw=f mry=f dbi
What his eldest and beloved son Debi **made** for him

Notes
i   *-n=f* precedes *sꜣ=f smsw=f mry=f* in word order.
ii In *sꜣ=f smsw=f mry=f* both *smsw* and *mry* share the following *=f* and the phrase means literally 'his son, his eldest, his beloved'.

In this book we shall focus on the relative form only when it shows the extra *-t*. In this way we can isolate the following convenient translation schemes for the past *sḏm.n(=f)* form and the past relative form *sḏmt.n(=f)* discussed in this chapter:

PAST TENSE   *ir.n=f*   he did

PAST RELATIVE FORM   *irt.n=f*   what he did

Excursus: Names and kinship terms

Names and family relationships play an important role on funerary stelae. We present here a number of the names to be found on the monuments studied in this book, and the kinship terms used, for you to refer to. As the section on names indicates, many Egyptian names (like our own) have a meaning. Nevertheless, in translating Egyptian monuments, it is better to stick to the name itself, rather than trying to translate the name into English.

Names
Names referring to personal condition
In a society with high infant mortality, it is not surprising that many names reflect anxiety about new-born children or wishes for their future health:

[glyph]	Senbi (Meir tomb-chapel B, No. 1)	*snbi*	healthy
[glyph]	Nakhti (BM EA 143)	*nḫti*	strong, vigorous
[glyph]	Khu (BM EA 571)	*ḫw*	protected

Names referring to deities
One type associates the individual directly with a deity:

[glyph]	Isis (BM EA 143)	*ꜣst*

A second type invokes a close – often familial – relationship with a god:

[glyph]	Sarenenutet (BM EA 585)	*sꜣ-rnnwtt*	son of Renenutet
[glyph]	Satsobek (BM EA 586)	*sꜣt-sbk*	daughter of Sobek
[glyph]	Senwosret (BM EA 571)	*s-n-wsrt*	man of the powerful one

A third type involves a pious statement in response to the child's birth:

[glyph]	Ptahhotep (BM EA 584)	*ptḥ-ḥtp*	Ptah is content
[glyph]	Inhuretnakht (BM EA 1783)	*inḥrt-nḫt*	Inhuret is strong

Loyalist names
Names which associate the individual with the king:

[glyph]	Intef (BM EA 581)	*intf*	11th dynasty nomen
[glyph]	Amenemhet (BM EA 587)	*imn-m-ḥꜣt*	12th dynasty nomen
[glyph]	Nebipusenwosret (BM EA 101)	*nb(=i)-pw-snwsrt*	Senwosret is my lord

The birth names of the kings themselves accord with the standard naming conventions. Hence Amenemhet means 'Amun is in front', i.e. Amun is guiding the child's fortunes (compare with Senwosret above).

Kinship terms

Stelae emphasise family relationships by naming members of the deceased's family and household (often including servants and dependants). The living members are usually shown presenting offerings to the offering-table, thus eternalising the offering cult to the deceased owner in stone. By including the various relatives and dependants on the monument of the deceased, these too enjoyed the benefits of being commemorated by figure and by name. Access to such monuments as funerary stelae was rather limited, mostly to those holding some form of élite position. The crucial relationship was that between the father and the eldest son: in social terms, this was the route of inheritance, providing family continuity; in cult terms, the eldest son was the chief celebrant for his father (as Horus was for Osiris).

Principal kinship terms:

![glyph] or ![glyph]	*it*	father	![glyph]	*mwt*	mother
![glyph]	*hi*	husband	![glyph]	*ḥmt*	wife
![glyph]	*sn*	brother	![glyph]	*snt*	sister
![glyph]	*s3*	son	![glyph]	*s3t*	daughter
![glyph]	*3bt*	family, household			

Family members are often referred to as being 'beloved'.

Label before one of the sons of Khuenbik offering fowl:

BM EA 584:
s3=f mry=f ptḥ-ḥtp
His son, his beloved, Ptahhotep

Sometimes, though, we find a more abbreviated writing.

Label before the first sons in the third row of BM EA 571:

BM EA 571:
s3=f mry=f imny
His son, his beloved, Ameny

(In idiomatic English we might prefer 'his beloved son'.)

The parentage of the owner is usually introduced by one of the two following phrases:

![glyph]   *ir-n*   born of   ![glyph]   *ms-n*   born of

Literally, *ir-n* means 'whom X made' and *ms-n* means 'whom X bore'. Usually *ir-n* is used of both the father and mother, whereas *ms-n* is used of the mother alone. When the person this phrase is applied to is feminine, both, as usual, show a ![glyph] *-t* (before ![glyph] *n*).

The name and filiation of the wife of Ameny on BM EA 162 (see Exercise 8.5):

BM EA 162

mdḥw mst-n imny mȝꜥt-ḥrw
Medhu born of Ameny, the justified

Properly speaking *ir-n* and *ms-n* are probably masculine relative forms – see §52 below. However, in this book we will stick to the distinctive transliteration using '-': *ir-n* and *ms-n*.

Exercises

5.1 Signs

<table>
<tr><td></td><td>*iw*</td><td></td><td>*ḥs*</td><td></td><td>*ḥkȝ*</td></tr>
<tr><td></td><td>*nm*</td><td></td><td>*dȝ*</td><td></td><td></td></tr>
</table>

5.2 Words
Transliterate the following words written with these signs:

....	favour, praise	....	friend
....	boat-journey	....	proceed, go, set out
....	ruler	....	amethyst
....	formal journey	....	wrong
....	ferry		

nmtt is the word used for the formal and festal journeys of the god and the king. It is a collective term and not a plural (and hence does not require (*w*) in transliteration despite the presence of plural strokes).

5.3 Translation
Transliterate and translate the following sentences. Some were used in the text above and so give you the chance to work through these examples thoroughly. You may wish to consult §35 on the omission of the pronoun =*i*.
a. Ikhernofret relates his role in the Mysteries of Osiris:

Berlin 1204, Line 18:

(The verb *ir(i)* 'to do' is used with a wide range of idiomatic meanings; here the sense is 'conduct'.)

b. The official Intef son of Senet proclaims his ethical behaviour:

BM EA 562, Line 10:

c. Inhuretnakht extols his proper conduct as a responsible official:

BM EA 1783, Line 4:

d. Another of Inhuretnakht's stated ethical acts (m added for clarity):

BM EA 1783, Lines 4-5:

e. Ity notes his success and achievement:

BM EA 586, Line 2:

For *e.* keep to a literal rendering of the Egyptian.

VOCABULARY

	iꜣ(w)	the old		*iwꜣ(w)*	cattle
	iww	the boatless		*ip*	inspect
	wḥm	repeat		*prt*	procession
	mẖnt	ferry		*nsw*	king
	ḥꜣy	the naked		*ḥḳr*	the hungry
	ḥr	before		*ḳrs*	bury
	ḏꜣ(i)	ferry		*ḏs=i*	myself, my own

5.4 Study exercise: BM EA 1783

In this exercise, you can make a start on studying a more complex stela in the British Museum: BM EA 1783, the stela of the governor Inhuretnakht and his wife Hui from Nagꜥ ed-Deir. The stela is shown on p. 74.

a. Transliterate and translate the offering formula at the top of the stela (Lines 1-2 ending with the word *ḏd* just before the end of Line 2), using the notes given.

b. Transliterate and translate the section starting at the beginning of Line 4 (we shall return to the section from the end of Line 2 to the end of Line 3 in Chapter 7).

The cemetery of Nagꜥ ed-Deir, opposite modern Girga, was the cemetery for Thinis (*ṯni*), the capital of the 8th Upper Egyptian nome (which also includes Abydos); *in-ḥrt* (Inhuret or Onuris) was its principal deity. Nagꜥ ed-Deir was an important cemetery centre from Predynastic times to the 11th dynasty and the start of the Middle Kingdom, at which time Thinis seems to have been eclipsed by Abydos.

BM EA 1783
(carved and painted limestone; H. 66cm)

BM EA 1783 dates from the First Intermediate Period and is a classic example of the regional Nagʿ ed-Deir style of that period, both in terms of its artwork and the conventional phraseology of the inscription, which is orientated around the family and ethical behaviour.

Notes

i ⬯ is a determinative of *prt-ḥrw*. See §26, p. 38

ii See Chapter 3 for the various titles of Inhuretnakht and the use of *imꜣḫw* 'the revered one'. Be careful with the title at the start of line 2.

iii Self-presentation inscriptions are usually cast as a speech, and are introduced by *ḏd* 'who says' or *ḏd=f* 'he says'.

iv See §35 for the omission of the first person pronoun.

v *ḏs(=i)* is used as the emphatic reflexive (as in 'I shall do that myself' or 'my own house').

vi Before *mẖnt* the preposition *m* 'in' has been omitted.

vii *ir(i)* 'do, make' is used here in the sense of 'acquire' or possibly 'raise'.

VOCABULARY

𓄿	*ꜣbt*	family, household		*iww*	the boatless
	im(ꜣ)	gracious, gentle		*in-ḥrt-nḫt*	Inhuretnakht
	it	father		*mwt*	mother
	mr(i)	love		*mẖnt*	ferry
	nb pt	lord of the sky		*ḥꜣy*	the naked
	ḥbsw	clothes		*ḥs(i)*	praise
	ḥḳr	the hungry		*snw snwt*	siblings, brothers and sisters
	kꜣ(w) 100	100 bulls		*ḏꜣ(i)*	ferry

The Family

c. Transliterate and translate the labels around the other family members. Hui has the following titles:

	ḫkrt nsw wʿtt	sole lady in waiting		*ḥm(t)-nṯr ḥwt-ḥr*	priestess of Hathor

The form of the kinship expressions are alike, although some writings exhibit sharing of elements:

ḥmt-f mrt=f   his beloved wife   sꜣ=f mry=f   his beloved son

sꜣ=f smsw=f   his beloved
mry=f   eldest son

NAMES

ḥwi   Hui   dbi   Debi   nnwy   Nenwy

5.5 Study exercise: BM EA 571 (top)

The top section of the stela of Khu and her two husbands, shown on p. 77.
a. Translate the offering formulae above the two scenes.

VOCABULARY

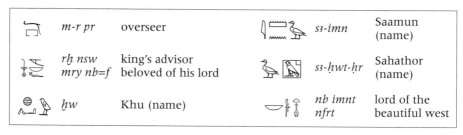

m-r pr	overseer	
rḫ nsw mry nb=f	king's advisor beloved of his lord	
ḫw	Khu (name)	
sꜣ-imn	Saamun (name)	
sꜣ-ḥwt-ḥr	Sahathor (name)	
nb imnt nfrt	lord of the beautiful west	

The second offering formula contains a different set of offerings:

mw   water   mrḥt   oil, unguent

ḥnḳt   beer   snṯr   incense

Festivals

The general word for a festival is *ḥb*:   or   ḥb   festival

The procession of Osiris to Poker: ḏꜣt nṯr   the god's boat-
                                             r pḳr   journey to Poker

A number of particular or periodic festivals are often mentioned on stelae.
The following is a list of the ones which appear on BM EA 571, arranged in
the typical order in which they occur:

ꜣbd   the monthly
      festival   ?-nt   the half-monthly
                               festival, i.e. full moon

wꜣg   the Wag-festival   ḏḥwtt   the Thoth-festival

The reading of the half-month festival is still unclear. An old suggestion to
read *smdt* has problems. More recently, the suggestion has been made that
the reading should be based around the number fifteen, as *mḏdint*.

The presence of the festivals on such stelae reflects the desire of the
deceased to partake in the offerings made before the god in the temples on

BM EA 571 (top)
(carved limestone; w. 51cm)

festival days; once the god had satisfied himself with them, they were passed on to the blessed dead. See the conclusion of the festival list on BM EA 162 in Exercise 8.5 for a further illustration of this point.

Offering bearers

b. Transliterate and translate the inscriptions accompanying the offering bearers in the two scenes. The inscriptions accompanying the two major offering bearers in the top scene fit the hieroglyphs around the figures. This can lead to unusual arrangements. They are given below in a conventional order:

accompanying the son   accompanying the overseer of the storehouse

VOCABULARY

¶ or ¶	*wbȝ*	cup-bearer, butler		*m-r st*	overseer of the storehouse
	m-sȝ=f	Emsaf (name)		*ḫnms=f mry(=f)*	his beloved friend
	sȝ-mnḫt	Samenkhet (name)		*sḥtp-ib*	Sehetepib (name, more fully Sehetepibre)

(Names ending with *m-sȝ=f* usually start with a god's name, as in *ḥr-m-sȝ=f* Horemsaf.)

5.6 Study exercise: BM EA 571 (bottom)

The bottom section of stela BM EA 571, shown on the following page, shows further family members and members of the household and estate staff.

a. Transliterate and translate the inscriptions. You may wish to make use of the Excursus on names and kinship.

b. Here are the names and titles in the scene. Some of the names are not transliterated. Transliterate them yourself:

NAMES AND TITLES

		Ameny		*sȝt-mnṯw*	Satmentju
	ṯȝw	Tjau		*sȝt-wsr(t)*	Satwosret
		Amenemhet		*bt*	Bet
	ḫw	Khu		*sȝ-ḥwtḥr*	Sahathor
	ddt	Dedet			Hetep
	s-n-wsrt	Senwosret		*ḥm-nṯr*	priest

OCCUPATIONS

🕊	*ꜥk(y)t*	entering-maid (literally, 'the enterer')	🏠	*ḥrt-pr*	domestic
🍶	*wbꜣt*	cup-bearer (fem.)	🦅	*sftw*	butcher
🦉	*rḫty*	washerman	🦅	*šmsw*	attendant

BM EA 571 (bottom)
(carved limestone; w. 51cm)

Further aspects of description

In this chapter, we will look at how complex descriptions are presented, in particular continuing to the next point and noting other things going on at that time.

Now is a good time for you to start using the Egyptian-English vocabulary (starting on p. 151), when reading the examples in the text.

§38 Continuation

Descriptions are often presented as a series of connected episodes. In past descriptions, as we saw in Chapter 5, the first episode is introduced by an auxiliary such as *iw*, then described by a verb in the past tense made up of the *sḏm.n(=f)* form. A past description is continued on simply by carrying on with the *sḏm.n(=f)* without any further introductory auxiliary. In translating such a series, it is useful to translate the following *sḏm.n(=f)*s with 'and ...' (there is no separate word for 'and' in Egyptian), or to use commas or semi-colons, depending on English style:

The official Intef son of Senet proclaims his ethical behaviour in general terms:

BM EA 562,   *iw   ḳrs.n=i iꜣ(w)*
Lines 10-11:   *ḥbs.n=i ḥꜣy*
               I buried the old
                  and I clothed the naked

Here the second past tense form ![glyph] *ḥbs.n=i* 'I clothed' carries on the description of Intef's ethical behaviour, rather than starting a new point. Notice how this gives a sense of shape and connection to episodes; for a clear example of the use of auxiliaries and *sḏm.n(=f)*s to give shape to description, see Exercise 6.5 below.

Sometimes elements are shared, just as in the English translation:

Inhuretnakht is extolling his proper conduct as a responsible official:

BM EA 1783,   ![glyphs]
Line 4:   *iw rdi.n(=i)   t n ḥḳr*
                           ḥbs n ḥꜣy

> I gave bread to the hungry
> > and clothes to the naked

⊏⊐(⧈) *rdi.n(=i)* 'I gave' is shared: 'I gave bread to the hungry and (I gave) clothes to the naked'.

Ity notes his success and achievement:

BM EA 586,
Line 2:

iw   wḥm.n(=i) ḥst ḥr nsw
sꜥꜣ ib(=i) r itw(=i) ḫprw r-ḥꜣt=i
I repeated favour before the king
> and advanced my heart further than my
> > forefathers who existed before me

Notes

i   ⧈.*n(=i)* 'I ..-(e)d' is shared: 'I repeated favour ... and (I) advance(d) my heart'.

ii   *r* 'to, in relation to' sometimes has the sense of 'more than'.

iii   *ḫprw* 'who existed' is a participle (see Chapter 7).

§39 Negation

The negative of the past ('I did not do that') is made up of the negative word ~ *n* followed by *sḏm(=f)* (it is not, as we might expect, formed by *n sḏm.n(=f)*!):

Following on immediately from his statement of positive ethical virtues (see above), Intef adds:

BM EA 562, Line 11:

n ir(=i) iwit r rmṯ
I did not do wrong against people (or: I did no wrong ...)

This negation also occurred in the opening scene to this book (notice the slightly stronger translation with 'never'):

Above the man roasting a goose:

Meir III, pl. 23:

n mꜣ=i mity srw pn
I have never seen the like of this goose

Sometimes the negation is written (rather confusingly!) with ~ .

The official Key notes his ethical virtues:

BM EA 558, Line 5:

n ḏws(=i) s n ḥry-tp=f
I did not denounce a man to his superior

Negations with ⌣ do not go with auxiliaries and so the pattern can either be used to start up or to carry on a series of connected episodes without any obvious written mark.

§40 Making someone do something (for use with Exercise 6.5)
Causation, the notion of 'making someone do something', is expressed in the following way in Egyptian: the verb *rdi* 'give, place' is used with the sense of 'causing' and is followed by another verb. *rdi* appears in whatever form is suitable (in the example below it appears in the past tense *sḏm.n(=f)* form) whilst the other verb appears in a fixed form (as it happens, the other verb appears in the future *sḏm(=f)*, for which see Chapter 8; however, this is not important at this point):

After the festivities are over, Ikhernofret has the image of the god placed back in the bark (see Exercise 6.5 for the general context of this example):

Berlin 1204,
Lines 21-22:

di.n=i wḏꜣ=f r-ḥnw wrt
I **had** him proceed inside the great bark
(literally, 'I caused that he proceed inside the great bark')

It may help to think of this as 'placing someone in the position to do something' or 'giving someone the opportunity to do something'; hence the example would mean: 'I put him (in the position) to proceed inside the great bark' or 'I facilitated his proceeding into the great bark'. The precise meaning can range from nuances of compulsion ('make someone do something') to permission ('allow/let someone to do something') and guidance ('have someone do something').

§41 Dependent pronouns
The second set of pronouns are the *dependent pronouns* (see Reference table, p. 149):

I		or		-wi or -w(i)		he/it		or		-sw
you		or		-ṯw or -tw		she/it		or		-s(y)

The major usage of the dependent pronouns are as the objects of verbs (typically the person or thing to which the verbal action is applied):

Tjetji records that, after Intef II died, he served the new king Intef III:

BM EA 614,
Line 13:

iw šms.n(=i) **-sw** *r s(w)t=f nbt nfrt nt sḫmḫ-ib*
I followed **him** to all his places of the heart's delight
(i.e. wherever the king wanted to go)

Notice that the suffix pronouns serve as subjects of the verb (see §§33 and 36) and dependent pronouns as objects of the verb.

The dependent pronouns display an important feature of word ordering: the dependent pronouns attach to and directly follow the verb and so *precede* any nouns:

The official Semti refers to his early favour at court:

BM EA 574,
Lines 2-3:

iw di.n **-wi** *ḥm=f r rdwy=f m nḫnt(=i)*
His person (i.e. the king) placed me at his feet in my youth

If you look carefully at this example, then *-wi* is a dependent pronoun and therefore should be the object of the verb (someone must have placed **me**) and so the sentence must mean that the king placed me at his feet, despite the order of the words. This sentence cannot mean: 'I placed the king at his feet in my youth' (for 'I' to be the subject, this would require the suffix pronoun *=i*) and in any case such a sentence scarcely makes much sense.

§42 The present tense

The monuments discussed in this book do not include many inscriptions cast in the present tense. However, for your information, and to allow us to cover one inscription we would otherwise have shown you but not equipped you to read, we will briefly note the present tense forms.

Middle Kingdom Egyptian distinguishes, just as English does, between a *general present* (usually expressing habit – She **goes** to visit her friend every week' – or things which just generally are – 'two and two **make** four') and a *specific or ongoing present* ('She **is leaving** right now'). In Middle Egyptian these have the following form (using *sḏm* to label the form and the weak verb *ir(i)* to exemplify it):

GENERAL PRESENT	SPECIFIC PRESENT
sḏm=f	*ḥr sḏm*
ir=f he does	*ḥr irt* (he) is doing

In the specific present, the verb appears after *ḥr* in the infinitive form discussed in Chapter 4. For a full list of forms, see the Reference tables on p. 145.

Both tenses have a fondness for the auxiliary *iw* introduced in §34 as illustrated by the examples below. They also share the same intricacies of usage as their English equivalents (for example, in Egyptian, as in English, verbs of state and condition prefer the general present to the specific present even when referring to things going on now: 'I know the answer now', not 'I am knowing the answer now'):

a. sḏm(=f)

To the left of the main offering formula inscription on BM EA 587:

BM EA 587:

iw wꜥb ḫꜣ m t ḥnḳt snṯr mrḥt
The thousand(s) of bread, beer, incense and oil are pure

b. ḥr sḏm

An example of this construction occurred in the first inscription shown to you in this book:

Above the man roasting a goose:

Meir III, pl. 23:

iw=i ḥr mꜥḳ ḏr pꜣt
I have been roasting since the beginning of time

Egyptian, like many languages, concentrates on the fact that the subject is continuing to roast despite the long time he has been doing it: 'I am still roasting and have been since the beginning of time'.

§43 Other things going on (advanced notes for use with Exercise 6.5)
However, there is one use of the present tense which will be useful when you study Exercise 6.5. In past description, as we have seen, the past events are described by using the past tense *sḏm.n(=f)* form. By stringing together a present *sḏm(=f)* form or *ḥr sḏm* form after a past *sḏm.n(=f)*, Egyptian expresses the notion of something else going on at the same time as that event expressed by the *sḏm.n(=f)* form (something else current or present at that time):

Ikhernofret relates his activities during the performance of the Mysteries of Osiris:

Berlin 1204,
Line 17:

*iw ir.n=i prt wp-wꜣwt **wḏꜣ=f** r nḏ it=f*
I conducted the procession of Wepwawet
when he **set out** to protect his father

Notes

i   *ir(i)* literally, 'to do/make', here with the sense of leading or conducting.

ii   *r nḏ* preposition + infinitive 'to protect'.

Notice that there is no Egyptian word for 'when', 'while', 'as' in these usages, although the appropriate English word may be needed in translation. In English, the notion of 'going on at the same time' is expressed by connecting words such as 'as', 'whilst', 'when'. In Egyptian it is the verb itself which expresses this by appearing in a present tense form (present or going on at that time). Indeed, you may have noticed that whereas in English connections are shown by words such as 'and' and 'as', in Egyptian the same meaning is achieved by stringing together different tenses such as *sḏm.n(=f)* and *sḏm(=f)* and letting the verbs do the work.

Exercises

6.1 Signs
2-consonant and 3-consonant signs:

	mi		*ḏr*		*ḥsf*
	nḏ		*ḳd*		*šms*

6.2 Words
Transliterate the following words written with these signs:

		since			like, as
	....	protect, save		....	drive away, repel
	....	the like, peer, equal		....	night of vigil
	....	sail		....	follow

6.3 Translation
Transliterate and translate the following (see §35 on omission of *=i* 'I').

The first one repeats examples from the chapter above and is written here without any breaks (as in the original inscription):

a. The official Intef son of Senet proclaims his ethical behaviour in general terms:

BM EA 562,
Lines 10-11:

b. Hekaib asserts his ethical behaviour:

BM EA 1671,
Lines 4-5:

This First Intermediate Period stela shows a number of idiosyncracies in the spelling, such as the form of *di* (instead of) and the form of the determinative for 'clothes'.

The final example is slightly more complex and is written in the right-to-left order of the original:

c. Tjetji describes his advancement by king Intef II:

BM EA 614,
Lines 4-5:

Notes

i -*w* is written for -*wi*.

ii Read *di.n=f* -*w(i)* in clause 3.

iii Also read ʿ*ḥ=f n wʿʿw*.

6.4 Translation

It has been a long time coming, but you are now in a position to read for yourself the speech of the man roasting the goose, which we used to begin this book. This is shown again below.

Notes

i On suffix pronouns, see §33 and §36.

ii On the *ḥr* + infinitive tense, see §42.

iii On negation, see §39.

VOCABULARY

	iwit	wrong		ʿ*3(w)*	the great
	ʿ*ḥ*	palace		*wʿʿw*	privacy
	p3t	the beginning of time		*pn*	this
	mʿk	roast		*nḏs(w)*	ordinary folk, the lowly
	rmṯ	people		*ḥbs*	clothe (verb)

VOCABULARY (CONTINUED)

𓄤	ḥry-tp	superior, chief	𓌟	sꜥꜣ	advance, promote
𓄿𓅬	srw	goose	𓋴𓂋𓐍𓅆	srḫ	complain about, accuse
𓏏𓎛𓈖𓏏	sḫnt	augment, promote	𓊪𓍿𓈎𓅆	skbḥ	put (someone) at ease
𓊨𓉐	st	place, position, status	𓏏𓎛𓂋𓏏𓄣	st ḥrt-ib	confidence

6.5 Study exercise: The Osiris Mysteries at Abydos

The celebration of the Mysteries of Osiris at Abydos was clearly one of the major festivals of Middle Kingdom Egypt. The festival centred around the burial and rejuvenation of Osiris, with its promise of burial and rejuvenation for the blessed dead. Indeed, as discussed in Chapter 4, a number of the élite erected stelae or cenotaphs in the area bordering the route to ensure their eternal participation in the rites.

The festival itself seems to have comprised five parts:

1   The first procession led by Wepwawet and culminating in combat against the enemies of Osiris. This seems to have been a celebration of kingship with the repelling of the forces of chaos and disorder (possibly reflecting the threat of disorder at the death of the old king Osiris – see p. 41 for the mythological account).

2   The great procession of Osiris himself. This seems to have been the start of the burial procession of Osiris as the dead king, when he was equipped and prepared for burial. Osiris here appeared in his form of Khentyimentu 'the one who is foremost of the westerners' and was taken out from the temple through the surrounding cemetery site.

3   The god's boat-journey to Poker. The god was conveyed in the great bark out into the desert to his supposed tomb at Poker (probably the tomb of King Djer of the First Dynasty at Umm el-Qaꜥab).

4   A night of vigil in which the god was rejuvenated as Wenennefer (see p. 42), including the Haker-festivities and a slaughter of the enemies of Osiris at Nedyet (the mythological place of his death). Unfortunately, this remains the most secretive and elusive part of the mysteries, though later accounts mention that Osiris was crowned with the crown of justification (𓌳𓂝𓏤𓊤𓅆 mꜣꜥ-ḫrw) and transfigured or enspirited (𓐍𓄿𓂝 sꜣḫ).

5   The return journey to Abydos among general rejoicing and the re-entry of the god into his temple.

The stela of the Treasurer Ikhernofret, now in Berlin, is one of the principal sources for the Osiris Mysteries. Ikhernofret was sent to Abydos by

Senwosret III to repair the image of the god and to perform the necessary ritual acts. He subsequently erected a stela in which he recounts how he organised the festival (an account which draws on previous versions given by earlier generations of officials sent by the Middle Kingdom kings to Abydos).

a. Transliterate and translate the following sections from the stela of Ikhernofret:

There follows a brief description of the manner in which Ikhernofret equipped the bark and put the proper regalia on the god, then:

The stela is unfortunately silent on the most mysterious features of the festivities such as the night of vigil and the Haker-festivities (compare with BM EA 567 in Study Exercise 8.3). There follows a description of the rejoicing along the route back, ending with the boat arriving at Abydos, then:

Notes

  i *r nḏ* preposition + infinitive, translate 'to protect'. On the writing of *it*, 'father', see Exercise 2.5: read here *it=f* 'his father'.

 ii You may find §43 helpful in translating *wḏꜣ=f* and *šms=i*.

iii You may find §27 on the direct and indirect genitive helpful.

 iv *ḏsr* as an adjective means 'sacred' (in *tꜣ ḏsr* 'sacred land') and as a verb means 'to clear (something) out'; in this text the verb is deliberately chosen to mark the transition of the festival from the public view to the hidden mysteries to take place at the tomb, and this happens once the procession has passed through *tꜣ ḏsr*.

  v See §40 on *di.n=i* followed by a verb to express causation.

 vi *hrw pf* 'that day', translate '(on) that day …'

vii The bark of Osiris is called the Neshmet-bark (*nšmt*) or else is simply referred to as the great bark (*wrt*); both are feminine words and are referred to by the feminine pronoun *=s* 'it' in *in.n=s* 'it brought' (for *in(i)* 'bring', see p.44). See the reference table on suffix pronouns on p. 148.

VOCABULARY

(for other words, see Egyptian-English Vocabulary, beginning on p. 151)

	it	father		*ꜥḥ*	palace, temple
	ꜥḥꜣ	fight, fighting		*wꜣ(w)t*	ways, roads
	wnn-nfr	Wenennefer (name of Osiris)		*wrt*	the great bark
	wḏꜣ	proceed, go, set out		*pf*	that
	pḳr	Poker		*mꜥḥꜥt*	tomb, often cenotaph
	nmtt	journey		*nšmt*	Neshmet-bark
	nṯr	god		*ndyt*	Nedyet
	nḏ	protect, save		*hrw*	day
	ḥr	(up)on, at		*ḫft(w)*	enemies
	ḫntt	(which is) at the forefront of		*ḫsf*	drive away, repel
	ḫnw	inside		*sbi(w)*	rebels, enemies
	sḫr	fell, overturn		*sḳd(i)*	sail, travel
	šms	follow		*ṯsw*	(sand)bank
	dpt-nṯr	the god's boat		*ḏsr*	separate, clear

EXTRA VOCABULARY

	ḥꜣkr	the Haker-festivities		*sḏrt*	night of vigil

b. Look at the episodes in this section from the stela of Ikhernofret and examine how *iw* and the past tense *sḏm.n(=f)* form are used to give shape to the passage. As a guide, note that in most instances, the auxiliary *iw* is followed not by one but by two or three past-tense verbs; only in the sentence beginning *iw ḏsr.n=i* is *iw* followed by a single verb. How does your grammatical account correlate with the different sections of the festival?

BM EA 586
(carved and painted limestone; H. 63.5cm)

6.6 Study exercise: BM EA 586

a. The stela on p. 90 is by no means an easy text, but with the help of the following notes, have a go at transliterating and translating the top section of this stela or use the key on p. 170 to work through it.

Notes

  i On dating and the titles of the king, see §§17-19. The king's cartouche is surmounted by the sky hieroglyph, which is not read.

  ii *wḥm ḥst* 'to repeat favour' with *wḥm* in the *sḏm.n(=f)* form. On the omission of *=i* 'I', see §35.

 iii *sꜥꜣ* 'to advance' (one's position, here 'heart') literally, 'to make great'. The full form would have been *sꜥꜣ.n=i*, see §38 on coordination and sharing. *r* has the sense here of 'more than'.

 iv *ḫprw* 'who existed' is a participle (see Chapter 7 for discussion).

  v The section beginning *iw ṭs.n* is another example of coordination, here dealing with the king's gift of a great seal (*ḫtm ꜥꜣ*) and a staff (*ꜣryt*) to Ity. *ṭs(i)* lit. 'to tie on', is used for the seal which the king tied around Ity's neck, but this precise meaning does not really go with the decorated staff which Ity was also given, so translate 'assign (to)'.

 vi *mi šps-nsw nb* 'just like any dignitary of the king' (which you might wish to put in brackets) goes with the first gift (the seal), and contrasts with the special gift of the staff (with which Ity is depicted in the lower scene). *šps-nsw* is a conventional designation.

 vii *swꜥbt* is a participle with feminine agreement with *ꜣryt* 'staff', translate '(which was) decorated'. See Chapter 7.

viii *it-nṭr* 'god's father'. In the Middle Kingdom, this seems to have been a title bestowing high rank and favour on an official, typically for performing special commissions for the king to do with the cult of the gods, and also legitimating him for this task. Perhaps here the title is directly connected to the episode of the king's assignment of the great seal and a staff to Ity.

 ix The text ends abruptly with the names of Ity and Iuri. The wife's name is separated off by a vertical bar.

VOCABULARY

	ꜣryt	staff		*iwri*	Iuri (name)
	ib	heart		*it(w)*	(fore-)fathers
or	*it-nṭr*	god's father		*ity*	Ity (name)
	wḥm	repeat		*nsw*	king
	r-ḥꜣt	before		*hbny*	ebony

VOCABULARY   (CONTINUED)

	ḥmt=f *mrt=f*	his beloved wife		*ḥst*	favour
	ḥsmn	amethyst		*ḫpr*	come into being, exist
	ḫpr-k3-rꜥ	Kheperkare (Senwosret I)		*ḫr*	before
	ḫtm	seal		*sꜥ3*	advance
	swꜥb	decorate		*šps-nsw*	dignitary of the king
	ṯs(i)	tie, knot		*ḏꜥm*	electrum

The family

b. Transliterate and translate the labels above the sons and daughters of Ity.

VOCABULARY: NAMES

	imn-m-ḥ3t	Amenemhet		*int=f*	Intef
	s3t-wsrt	Satwosret		*s3t-sbk*	Satsobek

You will be asked to study the inscription from the bottom scene at the end of Chapter 7.

Characterisation

*This chapter concentrates on the elaborate epithets which abound on stelae, particu-
larly epithets characterising the owner as having lived an ethical life or having
performed well in royal service. This will also allow us to introduce you to another
extremely common Egyptian verb-form – the participle. To start with, however, we
need to return to adjectives.*

§44 Adjectives

You have already been introduced to adjectives in §10. In Egyptian, these
follow and agree with the noun they describe. If the noun is feminine and
ends in -*t*, the adjective will also end in -*t*. To wrap up this topic properly, the
full list of endings are:

SG. MSC.		no special ending		*nfr*
SG. FEM.	▱	-*t*		*nfrt*
PL. MSC.	𓅭	-*w* or ø		*nfr(w)*
PL. FEM.	▱	-*t*		*nfrt*

(The plural can be written with or without the plural strokes ı ı ı; moreover,
the -*w* of the masculine plural agreement is often omitted in writing, leaving
no ending at all – this is indicated by the symbol ø in the table above.)

Compare the following examples showing feminine singular agreement and masculine plural agreement:

Ikhernofret relates his role in the Mysteries of Osiris:

Berlin 1204,
Line 18:

iw ir.n=i prt ꜥ3t
I conducted the **great** procession

*The top part of BM EA 101 has Nebipusenwosret adoring the gods. Behind the figure
of Nebipusenwosret:*

BM EA 101:

*dw3 3sir m ḥb(w)=f **nfrw** ḏt r nḥḥ*
Adoring Osiris in his **wonderful** festivals enduringly and repeatedly

§45 Adjectives used as nouns

Adjectives are typically used to describe other words, but they can be used on their own to mean 'a person/people with that particular quality'. For example, in English 'I am an **Egyptian**', means 'I am an **Egyptian person**' (not a soldier, or a donkey, or anything else!); compare also English expressions such as the 'the rich' and 'the poor'. In Egyptian this is rather common:

The official Intef, son of Senet, proclaims his ethical behaviour in general terms:

BM EA 562,
Lines 10-11:   *iw ḳrs.n=i i3(w) ḥbs.n=i ḥ3y*
I buried **the old** and I clothed **the naked**

However, in Egyptian, the adjective can be singular with the meaning 'a rich one/(some)one rich', whereas English prefers to add a rather general word such as 'someone' (so *ḥ3y* probably means more accurately 'someone naked' or 'the naked one').

If the idea is indefinite, abstract or general: 'anything good' or 'what is good', the feminine form of the adjective is used:

	nfrt	good (n.) 'what is good'	from		*nfr*	good, perfect
	bint	evil (n.) 'what is bad'	from		*bin*	bad

Key proclaims his own ethical behaviour:

BM EA 558,
Line 4:   *ink ḏd nfrt*
I was one who said **what is good**

Notes
  i For *ink* , see §49 below.
  ii *ḏd* is a participle meaning 'one who said', see §§48 and 49.

The meaning of the feminine form of the adjective as 'what is good' is similar to the meaning of the relative form mentioned in §37.

§46 Participles

The participles are special forms of the verb which have many of the qualities of an adjective, particularly because they can be used to qualify nouns.

There are two groups of participles: the present participle has the meaning '(one) who does something'; the past participle has the meaning '(one) who did something'. The forms of the participles in different verb classes are as follows:

	PRESENT OR INCOMPLETE			PAST OR COMPLETE		
STRONG	𓂝𓄿	*sḏm*	(one) who hears	𓂝𓄿	*sḏm*	(one) who heard
DOUBLING	𓅓𓄿𓄿	*mȝȝ*	(one) who sees	𓅓𓄿	*mȝ*	(one) who saw
WEAK	𓌳𓂋	*mrr*	(one) who loves	𓌳𓂋	*mr*	(one) who loved
EXTRA WEAK	𓂧𓂧	*dd* (no *r*)	(one) who gives	𓂋	*rdi* (with *r*)	(one) who gave

(Participles also sometimes have a -*w* ending.)

Basically, any verb other than a strong verb has a doubled consonant in the present participle but not in the past participle. In the case of strong verbs, however, it is not possible to tell the two apart on the basis of their forms alone. As you will see in the examples below, there is no need in Egyptian for a separate word meaning 'who' (or 'which' or 'what') since this is an integral part of the meaning of the Egyptian participle verb-form.

§47 Participles and epithets

Since a participle behaves a lot like an adjective, it is often used to qualify a noun. For example, participles are commonly used in the epithets characterising an official:

The stela of Ameny identifies his subordinate, Sahathor, with the epithet:

BM EA 162,   *bȝk=f   mȝʿ n st-ib=f*
Central column: ***irr** ḥsst=f rʿ nb*
                 His true servant of his affection,
                     who does what he favours every day

(*ḥsst=f* 'what he favours' is a present relative form, see §52 below.)

In the first part of this example both *mȝʿ* 'true' and *n st-ib=f* 'of his affection' help to characterise *bȝk=f* 'his servant'. Similarly in the second half of the example, *irr* is the present participle ('who does') and is also used to elaborate the character of *bȝk=f* 'his servant'.

Just like an adjective, a participle must agree with the noun it describes and so will end with ⌒ -*t* if the noun is feminine:

Before the figure of Medehu, the wife of Ameny:

BM EA 162,
Left column: *ḥmt=f mrt=f **irrt** ḥsst=f rꜥ nb*
His wife, beloved of him, **who does** what he favours every day

In this example, *irrt* ('who does') agrees with *ḥmt* 'wife'; for *mrt* 'beloved', see §50, below.

Alternatively, a participle may show an extra ⸜ -*w* with masculine plurals:

Ity asserts that he advanced himself more than:

BM EA 586,
Line 2:   *it(w)=i **ḫprw** r-ḥꜣt=i*
my (fore-)fathers who **existed** before me

§48 Participles as nouns

Again, like adjectives, participles can be used on their own to mean 'a person who does something' or more succinctly 'one who does something'. For example, BM EA 614 (the stela of Tjetji) introduces Tjetji himself with a long list of his titles and epithets, including:

BM EA 614,   *rḫ ḥrt-ib nb=f*
Line 1:   *šms -sw r nmtt=f nb*
one who knows the desire of his lord,
one who follows him at all his journeys

(For vocabulary, see p. 106.)

In this example, *rḫ* and *šms* are participles used on their own to mean '(a person) who knows' and '(a person) who follows'.

Incidentally, the participle is the form used in the name of Wepwawet, 'the one who opens the ways' (compare this with his role in the Osiris Mysteries studied in Exercise 6.5):

wp-wꜣwt   Wepwawet

(Participles used on their own sometimes translate well as an English agentive noun ending in '-er', here 'the opener of the ways'.)

§49 Characterisation with ○ *ink*

This construction is typically used to characterise someone as the type of person with certain qualities or attributes; in effect, it answers the question 'what was I like?', 'who was I?', focusing on ethical behaviour and success and achievement:

The self-presentation section of the stela of Hekaib begins in the following way:

BM EA 1671,
Line 1:   *ink nḏs iḳr*
                       I was an astute individual

ink is the 'I'-form (first person) of a third and last type of pronoun, called the *independent pronoun* because it can come at the beginning of a statement:

... or ...	*ink* I	Independent pronoun, written with the D33 pot, read here as *in*.

Notice that in this example there is no word for 'was' in this construction (the statement could also be translated in the present tense, i.e. 'I am an astute individual', but here the past tense seems appropriate to the idea of an official looking back over a life presented as now ended).

    It is not unusual to find the use of qualifying expressions such as participles:

The self-presentation of Hekaib continues:

BM EA 1671,   *ink nḏs iḳr*
Line 1:   *ḏd m r=f*
                I was an astute individual,
                who spoke with his (own) mouth

The owner is referred to the second time in the third person: ≈ *=f*, moving from the specific individual to a generalized social characterisation by characterising the first person 'I' (specific individual) in generalized third person terms ('one who spoke with his own mouth').

    In this example, the adjective (... *iḳr* 'astute') and the participle (... *ḏd* 'who spoke') both qualify ... *nḏs*. Often, however, *ink* is followed by a participle used on its own, to create a statement which means 'I was someone who did' (when using the past participle):

The official Key makes a common statement about appropriate behaviour:

BM EA 558,
Line 4:   *ink ḏd nfrt*
                I was **one who said** what is good

This *characterisation* construction tells us about what he was like. It does not mean 'I said what is good' – this would be a description, using the past tense *sḏm.n(=f)* form, and would tell us about what he did, rather than what he was like:

A made-up example to illustrate the point in the text:

iw *ḏd.n=i* nfrt
I **said** what is good

The two constructions differ clearly in form and also in meaning, just as their English translations do.

§50 Passive participles

Participles can either be active ('one who loved') or passive ('one who was (be)loved'). Unfortunately, the passive participles do not usually have a distinctive writing in Egyptian. However, the most common examples in our inscriptions concern the verbs ⳾ *mr(i)* 'love' and ⳾ *ḥs(i)* 'favour' which, as weak verbs, in the past passive participle do sometimes show a distinctive ⳾ –*y* ending in the past passive participle. Since this is a rather common usage, we will discuss the point in some detail:

Inhuretnakht declares his status within his family:

BM EA 1783,
Lines 2-3:   ink **mry n** it=f
I was **one beloved** of his father

In such a usage, the passive participle is often followed by the genitive 'of', either the indirect genitive (as in the last example) or the direct genitive:

Tjetji declares his status in relation to the king:

BM EA 614,
Line 3:   ink **mry** nb=f
I was **one beloved** of his lord

The passive participle may even be followed by a suffix pronoun:

The stela of Tjetji continues:

BM EA 614,
Line 3:

ink mry nb=f
    ḥsy=f m ẖrt-hrw nt rꜥ -nb
I was one beloved of his lord
    and **favoured of him** (or, 'his favoured one')
        in the course of every day

In expressions of familial affection,   *mr(i)* sometimes occurs in the present/incomplete participle form   *mrrw*. The reason for this is still much discussed and may have to do with the presence of the following plural genitive expression. However, a much easier way to understand this in the next example is to note that that the previous generation (the owner's mother and father) take the past passive participle, whereas his siblings (i.e. the present generation from his point of view) take the present passive participle:

Inhuretnakht's full declaration of his status within his family (this completes Study Exercise 5.4):

BM EA 1783,
Lines 2-3:
ink mry n it=f ḥsy n mwt=f mrrw snw=f snwt=f im(ꜣ) n ꜣbt=f
I was one beloved of his father, praised of his mother, beloved of
    his siblings, and one gracious of/to his household

As an alternative, *mrrw* might be translated as a masculine relative form – see §52 below – and the translation reshaped: 'one whom his siblings love and one gracious to his household'.

Finally, you have already encountered the past passive usage on a number of occasions in various labels of filiation. A particularly good example occurs on BM EA 584, to be studied in Chapter 8:

Label before one of the sons of Khuenbik offering fowl:

BM EA 584:
sꜣ=f mry=f ptḥ-ḥtp
His son, his beloved, Ptahhotep

Often, though, we find a more abbreviated writing:

Label before the first sons in the third row of BM EA 571:

BM EA 571:
sꜣ=f mry=f imny
His son, his beloved, Ameny

(In idiomatic English we might prefer 'his beloved son'.)

§51 *in* + noun + participle

The participles are also used in a construction introduced by *in: in* + noun + participle 'it is so-and-so who did'. Like its English equivalent, this construction highlights the person who performs an action. It occurs quite commonly in a dedication formula which identifies the donor of a stela:

The label above Niptahkau on the stela dedicated to his father Khuenbik (see Chapter 8, pp. 122-3):

BM EA 584:   *in s₃=f sʿnḫ rn=f m-r iḳdw n-ptḥ-k₃w*
It is his son who made his name live (on),
the overseer of builders Niptahkau

§52 Relative forms again

In §37 above we introduced you to the past relative form. The relative form is in fact similar in usage to the participle. First of all, here is a table of the forms of the relative forms in the present and the past. As with the previous section on the relative form §37, we shall exhibit the form with a *-t* (although, as you will see, this is actually the *-t* of feminine agreement):

PRESENT OR INCOMPLETE

STRONG		*sḏmt=f*	what he hears
DOUBLING		*m₃₃t=f*	what he sees
WEAK		*mrrt=f*	what he loves
EXTRA WEAK		*ddt=f*	what he gives

PAST OR COMPLETE

STRONG		*sḏmt.n=f*	what he heard
DOUBLING		*m₃t.n=f*	what he saw
WEAK		*mrt.n=f*	what he loved
EXTRA WEAK		*rdit.n=f*	what he gave

(Compare with the forms of the participles in §46 above.)

In particular, like participles, relative forms display certain adjectival qualities. Thus they agree with the noun they accompany, for example taking a *-t* when going with feminine words. A good example occurs in the offering formula:

The offering formula in BM EA 558:

BM EA 558,
Line 2: *ḫt -nbt nfr(t) wꜥb(t) ꜥnḫt nṯr im*
everything good and pure on **which** a god **lives**

Also, just like adjectives, the relative forms show this helpful extra ⌒ -*t* when used on their own with the meaning '**what** someone does/did':

The stela of Ameny identifies his subordinate, Sahathor, with the epithet:

BM EA 162,   *bꜣk=f   mꜣꜥ n st-ib=f*
Central column: *irr ḥsst=f rꜥ nb*
His true servant of his affection,
            who does **what he favours** every day

Masculine relative forms do not show such a ⌒ -*t* and thus are harder to spot. Fortunately they are also fairly uncommon and need not concern us in this book. As noted in Chapter 5, p. 71, the filiation expressions for males *ir-n* and *ms-n* may well be examples of masculine relative forms.

Excursus: Middle Kingdom titles
In Chapter 3, various titles were introduced to provide you with a resource for your reading. In these notes, the titles are gathered together according to their function, to provide another convenient reference resource (the list includes some titles from other stelae in the British Museum).

General terms
Generic terms for office holding and status amongst the élite include the following:

or	*iꜣt*	office	*sr*	official
	bꜣk	servant	*nḏs*	individual

The term   *iꜣt* is the general term for a regular office or function. Such an office brought status, position and power, and also wealth through its attached estate (*pr*). The term   *bꜣk* 'servant' was often used as a means of stressing the dependent relationship of one person on another and could be used of people who otherwise had high status.   *nḏs* 'individual' was often used, particularly in the First Intermediate Period, for someone of high status who did not hold an official position.

The palace and the king

The 'palace' was an itinerant community gathered round the king, who, as well as residing at a central residential and administrative complex, also moved about the country in order to celebrate the festivals of Egypt's many gods. Officials would regularly visit the palace in order to renew their attendance on the king, before returning to the various regions to exercise their delegated authority.

Titles proclaiming attendance at court

	šmsw pr ꜥꜣ	follower of the palace		or	*rḫ nsw*	royal intimate, king's adviser

Titles associated with the ritual appearances of the king are usually compounded with the word *nsw* for 'king'.

Titles proclaiming attendance on the king

	iry nfr-ḥꜣt	keeper of the royal diadem		*imy-ḫnt*	chamberlain (the one in front)

Titles proclaiming rank and authority delegated from the king

	ḫtmty bity	king's seal-bearer		*smr wꜥty*	sole companion

Administrative titles are compounded with the word *bity* for 'king'. *ḫtmty-bity* is prefixed only to high-level titles. As well as signifying high rank, the title indicated that the holder was authorised to use the royal seal.

The treasury

For the monuments studied in this book, the officials attached to the treasury have particular importance:

Procurement, storage, dispensing and utilisation

	m-r ḥtmt	treasurer (overseer of what is sealed)		*m-r ꜥḫnwty*	overseer of the chamber
	ḫtmw ḥry-ꜥ	seal-bearer, assistant (to the treasurer)			

The title *m-r ꜥḫnwty* was originally more general. In origin it probably referred to the 'overseer of the chamber of the residence/palace'. However, by the Middle Kingdom the title had become split between a number of different branches of the administration. A particularly common *m-r ꜥḫnwty* 'overseer of the chamber' was the *m-r ꜥḫnwty n m-r ḥtmt* 'overseer of the chamber for the treasurer', who seems to have been responsible for the procurement of raw materials (for example through mining) and for monumental building work.

Stewardship and production

	m-r pr	overseer of the estate (steward)
	m-r iḳdw	overseer of builders
	m-r šnʿ(w)	overseer of the provisioning areas

Regional authority

Titles associated with the government of regional districts:

	ḥꜣty-ʿ	governor, mayor of a town		*wḥm(w)*	reporter, herald

Military

	m-r mšʿ wr	general-in-chief
	ʿnḫ n nwt	soldier of the town regiment

Religious titles

Titles associated with priestly functions. In the Middle Kingdom, there were few full-time priests, but élite men regularly served in the temples:

	wʿb	*wʿb*-priest	or	*it nṯr*	god's-father
	ḥm nṯr	*ḥm*-priest		*ḥm kꜣ*	*ka*-priest
	ḥry sštꜣ	Keeper-of-secrets		*ḥry ḥbt*	lector priest

Although we have divided secular and religious titles for convenience here, in practice these were intertwined in élite Middle Kingdom society, where the same person could hold both secular and religious titles at once. BM EA 585, where Sarenenutet has the following titles, provides an example of this:

	ḥsb šnwty	counter of the double granaries
	dd ḥtp(w)-nṯr n nṯrw	offering-giver to the gods

Titles of women

In general women were not included in the formalisation of élite society through office holding, which tended to be a male preserve (you may already have noted that most women depicted on the stelae in this book are usually referred to by their family relationship with the male owner). However, some women are shown bearing a certain range of titles which usually accord with the status of their menfolk. Of particular note for the stelae studied in this book are those of high status:

High status

ḥm(t)-nṯr ḥwt-ḥr   priestess of Hathor

ẖkrt nsw wᶜtt   sole lady in waiting

(*ẖkrt-nsw* means literally 'the king's ornament'.)

Another common title of élite women associates them with the running of the estate. It appears on stelae from the late 12th dynasty onwards:

Estate and household

nbt pr   lady of the house, mistress of the estate

Exercises

7.1 Signs
a. 2-consonant and 3-consonant signs

wḏ   ḫt   nḏm

mꜣ   ẖr

b. Ideograms and determinatives

SIGN		EXAMPLE		
	E58 – sail		ṯꜣw	breath
or	A10/A11 – man of rank on chair with/without flail		šps	dignified, august, rich
	E10 – emblem erected outside the temple of Min	or	iꜣt	office, function
	D18 – village with crossroads		nwt	town
	A7 – man holding stick and kerchief		sr	official

7.2 Words
Transliterate the following words written with these signs:

....   sweet   ....   create

....   under, carrying   ....   command (see also §21)

....   strong, vigorous

7.3 A note on the writing of ir(i) 'to do'

A major exception to the rule on sound complements given in Chapter 2 is provided by the verb ⌐ *ir(i)* 'to do, make' (this verb also has many idiomatic meanings). When read *ir*, it is generally written ⌐ alone (an exception occurs on BM EA 558 in Study Exercise 7.7 where, for space reasons, ⌐ seems to be written for *irr*), while ⌐ is usually to be transliterated *irr* (a third form, ≋, should always be transliterated *irr*):

⌐ *ir*	⌐ *irr*, more rarely *ir*	≋ *irr*

7.4 Translation

Transliterate and translate the following.

a. The self-presentation section of the stela of Hekaib begins in the following way, stressing the topic of self-reliance (you may consider adding 'own' in your translation to help bring this out), compare with §49 above:

BM EA 1671,
Lines 1-2:

Notes

i The hieroglyphs are organised as they are on the original, except that the elements of the passage are separated out for your convenience. You may find that you need to insert 'and' occasionally in your translation.

ii The pronoun =*f* is used to refer back to the owner of the stela as noted in §49 (as in: '**I** was an official well respected in **his** district' or the like). The switch to the third person is normal in such constructions.

iii *shsf ... r* 'to keep (something) at a distance from', idiom of impartiality.

iv *iwn ꜥꜣ* 'great pillar' is used metaphorically (cf. our own expression for someone being 'a tower of strength' or a 'pillar of the community')

v On the omission of the suffix pronoun =*i* 'I' in writing in the third sentence, see §35 above. Read *mity nb m nwt tn*.

b. The stela of Tjetji begins with the king's name and then Tjetji is introduced with a list of epithets:

BM EA 614,
Line 1:

Notes

  i   ⟳ is an early form of the papyrus roll ⟳. Another variant form is ⟳ .

  ii   On the dependent pronoun *-sw*, see §41.

7.5 *Stela of Ity (BM EA 586)*

Transliterate and translate the following, which is the lower section of the stela given as Exercise 6.6:

BM EA 586 (lower section)

Notes

  i   Notice the writing of the title *it-nṯr* 'god's father' (cf. Exercise 6.6).

  ii   Read *mry nb=f mꜣꜥ* 'one truly beloved of his lord', where *mry* is a participle (see §50 above). *nb=f* is placed first through prestige (see §22).

VOCABULARY

	iwn	pillar		*imn-rꜥ*	(the god) Amun-Ra
	it-nṯr	god's father (priestly title)		*ity*	Ity (name)
	wꜣst	Thebes (place)		*pr*	house, estate
	mity	peer, equal		*nmtt*	journeys
	r	mouth		*ḥry-sštꜣ*	master of secrets (title)
	ḥpš	strong arm		*ḫntyt*	Khentyt (place-name)
	ḫnt(y) st	(one) foremost of position		*ḫrt-ib*	desire
	sꜣt	daughter		*sꜣt-wsrt*	Satwosret (name)

VOCABULARY   (CONTINUED)

~ 𓊃𓏏𓆇	*sȝt-sbk*	Satsobek (name)	𓇋𓏏𓄿𓊖	*swȝ*	to pass by, surpass
𓏺𓎡𓄹	*sḫsf*	to keep at a distance	𓊃𓎶	*st*	place(s)
𓀻𓏺	*šps*	dignitary (literally, 'august one')	𓀻𓏤𓏤𓄑	*špss*	dignity, wealth

7.6 Relative forms

The relative forms are used in a common late Middle Kingdom addition to the offering formula, which occurs on BM EA 143, the stela of Nakhti to be studied in Exercise 7.8:

The voice-offering can be extended after 'everything good and pure on which a god lives' as follows:

BM EA 143,
Line 2:   𓊃𓄿𓅨𓈖𓏌𓇋𓅱𓈖𓏥𓎟𓏏

Notes

i   Remember that since these are relative forms, they will require translating here with 'which'. Also consult the table in §52 for the writings.

ii   See stela BM EA 143, Exercise 7.8, for vocabulary.

7.7 Study exercise: BM EA 558

The stela of Key on page 108 comes across as something of a compendium of standard expressions, rather than a smooth-running composition. Some of the sections of this inscription have already been used as examples in the main text. Transliterate and translate the stela with the help of the notes.

Notes

i   For the epithets, see §§47 and 50 above.

ii   For *ii m*, read *ii(.n=i) m*, parallel to *hȝ.n=i m*. Translate *m* as 'from'.

iii   For the omission of the suffix pronoun =*i*, see §35 above.

iv   For *ink* + participle, see §49 above.

v   *mrrt* is probably a present relative form, see §52 above.

vi   For the writing of the negative 𓂜 *n* as 𓈖, see §38 above (in both *n ḏws(=i)* and *n wḏ(=i)*).

vii   The expression *n wḏ(=i) ḥwt m s=i* is not without its difficulties. In English idiom, you may wish to translate *m* as 'for/to'.

viii   There is some doubt as to whether *whm* should be read as a title or as part of a name *wḥm-ky*.

This inscription also introduces the important verb 'to come':

'come' – written in two forms:

𓈐𓏌𓃀 , 𓈐𓅬   *iy(i)/iw(i)*   a. with monogram of 𓇋 *i* and 𓈐 walking legs
                                        b. with walking legs ideogram

BM EA 558
(carved and painted limestone; H. 80cm)

VOCABULARY

	wḥm(w)	reporter, herald (title: one who repeats)		*wḥm*	repeat
	wḏ	command		*mrti*	Merti (name)
	nsw	king		*rꜥ nb*	every day
	rḫ-nsw	king's adviser (title)		*hꜣ(i)*	descend, go down
	ḥwt	beating		*ḥry-tp*	chief, superior
	ḫrp rḫ-nsw	director of king's advisers		*ḫrt-hrw*	course of the day
	s	man		*spꜣt*	district
	ky	Key (name)		*ḏws*	denounce

7.8 Study exercise: BM EA 143

Transliterate and translate the stela of Nakhti (BM EA 143) on p. 110. You may wish to make use of your work for Exercise 7.6.

VOCABULARY

	ꜣst	Iset, Isis (name)		*in(i)*	bring
	pt	sky, heavens		*mwt=f*	his mother
	mnꜥt	wet-nurse		*ms-n*	born of
	nbt pr	lady of the house		*nḫti*	Nakhti (name, both male and female)
	nt-nbw	Netnebu		*nḏm*	sweet
	ḥꜥpy	the inundation (as the god Hapy)		*ḥmt=f*	his wife
	snṯr	incense		*kmꜣ*	create
	st	smell, scent		*ṯꜣw*	breath

Notes

i   Translate *m* near the end of Line 3 as 'as' (an elaboration into three parts: offering, breath and incense).

ii   In the writing of Abydos and Djedu the town determinative ⊗ has been expanded as though it were the word nwt 'town'. However, it is still simply the determinative for Abydos and Djedu, not a separate word.

iii In the first column of women, the first sign is a writing of ⊃ *ḥm*.

iv   This stela shows a number of features which place its date rather late in
the sequence of stelae studied in this book. The word for Djedu is written with two *ḏd*-signs, suggesting a date of at least the late 12th
dynasty. This is confirmed by the use of *n kȝ n* without *im3ḫ(w)* (see
§26) and by the use of the *ḏdt pt*-formula. It is thought that the 'breath-
of-life' formula only came into use in the 13th dynasty; if so, this would
suggest a date in the early 13th dynasty for this stela.

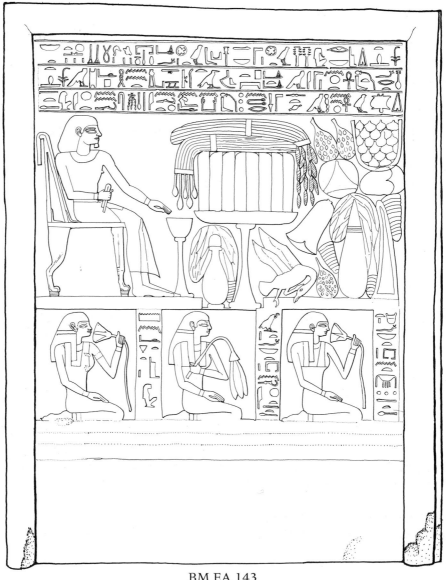

BM EA 143
(carved and painted limestone; H. 81.2cm)

Chapter 8

The future

In this final chapter, we will introduce you to the 'appeal to the living' formula in which the deceased calls upon future generations to maintain his funerary cult. We will also look at the future tense used particularly to express wishes and expectations.

§53 The *sḏmty.fy* form

In expressing the future, the place of the participle is taken by the *sḏmty.fy* form: '(someone) who will/may do something'. This form has the same uses as the participles, but has its own particular endings. In its fullest writings the *sḏmty.fy* form displays the following forms:

MASCULINE	FEMININE	PLURAL (BOTH GENDERS)
sḏmty.fy	*sḏmty.sy*	*sḏmty.sn*

Often, however, the ⟍ -*y* of the endings is omitted:

The stela of Mentjuhotep in the Fitzwilliam Museum, Cambridge, has an appeal to the living which begins:

Fitz.E9.1922,
Line 1:
ỉ ꜥnḫw tpw tꜣ swꜣt(y).sn ḥr is pn
O the living upon the earth **who may pass** by this tomb

(See §54 below for the form of the appeal to the living and its vocabulary.)

As with participles, the *sḏmty.fy* form can be used with a noun (in this example, *swꜣt(y).sn* 'who may pass' goes with 'the living') or on its own ('someone who will do something').

§54 The appeal to the living

The *appeal to the living* formula is found on many stelae. A simple example is:

The appeal to the living of the chamberlain Minnefer (year 29 of Amenemhet II):

BM EA 829,
Lines 4-5:

i ꜥnḫw tpw tꜣ ḥm(w)-nṯr ḥm(w)t-nṯr wꜥbw nw r-pr pn
ḏd=tn ḥꜣ t ḥnkt kꜣ ꜣpd n imꜣḫ(w) m-r ꜥḥnwty mnw-nfr mꜣꜥ-ḫrw
O living ones upon the earth, the *ḥm*-priests and *ḥm*-priestesses,
    and the *wꜥb*-priests of this temple,
may you say, 'A thousand (of) bread, beer, ox and fowl for the
    revered one, the overseer of the chamber Minnefer, the justified'

(See the Reference table on p. 148 for the suffix pronoun =*tn* 'you'.)

    The appeal to the living is composed of two basic elements plus a further, optional element:

a. Hailing the visitor

The owner of the memorial addresses the passers-by; the visitors are hailed, typically in the form:

As we saw above, the stela of Mentjuhotep begins with an appeal to the living:

Fitz.E9.1922,
Line 1:

i ꜥnḫw tpw tꜣ ...
O the living upon the earth ...

This is composed of the following words:

or	*i*	O	or	*tpw* (who are) upon
ꜥnḫw the living			*tꜣ* the earth	

(On the form of *tpw* 'upon', see §60 below.)

    There may follow an enumeration of the people likely to pass by – such as temple staff and scribes – who are often hailed in passing the monument:

The stela of Mentjuhotep continues:

Fitz.E9.1922,
Line 1:

*i ꜥnḫw tpw tꜣ **swꜣt(y).sn** ḥr is pn*
O the living upon the earth **who may pass** by this tomb

As in this example, in hailing the visitor, the verb *swꜣ* 'to pass' (*ḥr* 'by') is typically used in the *sḏmty.fy* form: *swꜣty.sn* '(they) who shall pass'. *swꜣ* can be written in the following ways:

FULLER WRITINGS   ABBREVIATED WRITINGS

    or   or   *swꜣ* pass (by)

(Note the abbreviated writings with × D7 crossed sticks.)

b. The offering request

The owner requests that offerings or prayers be made or said for him:

From BM EA 829:

BM EA 829,
Line 5:

ḏd=tn ḫꜣ t ḥnḳt kꜣ ꜣpd n imꜣḫ(w) m-r ꜥḥnwty mnw-nfr mꜣꜥ-ḫrw
May you say, 'A thousand bread, beer, ox and fowl for the revered
one, the overseer of the chamber Minnefer, the justified'

The request for saying the offering formula uses the future *sḏm(=f)* form discussed below in §55.

c. The appeal to goodwill or piety

The appeal to the living is often augmented by a third element – an invocation of the goodwill or piety of the visitors, or a declaration of the benefits visitors will gain if they make the offering. Sometimes this is included in hailing the visitors in the form of participles:

The appeal to the living of the priest Mentuhotep:

Fitz.F9.1922,
Line 1:

i ꜥnḫw tpw tꜣ swꜣty.sn ḥr is pn
    mrrw ꜥnḫ msḏḏw ḫpt
ḏd=tn sꜣḫ ꜣsir ḫnty-imntw mnṯw-ḥtp
O living ones upon the earth who may pass by this tomb
    and **who love** life and **who hate** death,
may you say, 'May Osiris Khentyimentu transfigure Mentjuhotep'

(mrrw and msḏḏw are both participles; see §46 above.)
    Often, however, the appeal to the goodwill or piety of the visitor takes the form of a separate clause (here beginning *m + mrr=tn*) leading on to the request to say the offering:

The appeal to the living of the overseer of builders Khuenbik:

BM EA 584,
Lines 3-5:

i ꜥnḫw swꜣt(y).sn ḥr mꜥḥꜥt tn m ḥd m ḫsft
m mrr=tn šms wp-wꜣwt r nmtt=f nb
ḏd=tn t ḥnḳt ......

O living ones who may pass by this cenotaph in going north or in
    going south,
as you wish to follow Wepwawet at his journeys,
may you say, 'Bread and beer ...'

Grammatically, the first clause is sometimes introduced by ⟨glyph⟩ *m* 'as' and the
request clause sometimes by ⟨glyph⟩ *mi* ('just as ..., so you should say ...')

§55 Wishes, expectations and requests: the future *sḏm(=f)*

The form used to express wishes, requests, expectations and the like is the
future *sḏm(=f)*. In the appeal to the living, you have already, in fact, encountered the future *sḏm(=f)* form of ⟨glyph⟩ *ḏd* ('say'):

The appeal to the living of the chamberlain Minnefer once more:

⟨hieroglyphs⟩

BM EA 829,   *i ꜥnḫw tpw tꜣ ḥm(w)-nṯr ḥm(w)t-nṯr wꜥbw nw r-pr -pn*
Lines 4-5:   ***ḏd=tn*** *ḥꜣ t ḥnkt kꜣ ꜣpd n imꜣḫ(w) m-r ꜥḥnwty mnw-nfr mꜣꜥ-ḫrw*
    O living ones upon the earth, the *ḥm*-priests and *ḥm*-priestesses,
      and the *wꜥb*-priests of this temple,
    may you say, 'A thousand (of) bread, beer, ox and fowl for the
      revered one, the overseer of the chamber Minnefer, the justified'

The future *sḏm(=f)* is a form distinct from the present *sḏm(=f)* noted in §42
above (although the two can be difficult to distinguish by the writings
alone). The future *sḏm(=f)*, for example, is not used with auxiliaries such as
iw. Its full forms are given in §59 below (you may wish to compare the writings of the two forms in the reference tables on pp. 145 and 146).

§56 The Abydos formula

The Abydos formula is a fairly standardised set of afterlife wishes. The
mature version belongs to the first half of the 12th dynasty with earlier (less
standardised) versions occurring in the 11th dynasty. The full formula has
twenty elements (as in BM EA 567), but many texts contain a selection:

A brief version of the Abydos formula occurs on BM EA 162:

BM EA 162,   ⟨hieroglyphs⟩
Lines 4-6:

⟨hieroglyphs⟩

    di.t(w) *n=f ꜥwy m nšmt ḥr wꜣ(w)t imntt*
    šsp=f *ḥtpt ḥr ḥtp ꜥꜣ m ḥb(w) n ḫrt-nṯr*
    ḏd.t(w) *n=f iw m ḥtp in wrw n ꜣbḏw m wꜣg m ḏḥwtt ...*

> **May** hands/help **be given** to him in the Neshmet-bark on the ways of the west;
>
> **May he receive** offerings on the great altar on the festivals of the necropolis;
>
> **May** 'Welcome in peace' **be said** for him by the great of Abydos: on the Wag-festival and on the Thoth-festival ... (a list of festivals follows)

(*.t(w)*) is the affix of the passive with *in* used for 'by' ('may something be done by someone').

You will be studying this formula in the Exercises to this chapter.

§57 Purpose and causation

a. Purpose/result clauses

The future *sḏm(=f)* is also used to express purpose or result ('so that', 'in order that'). This is the form used in the offering formula:

The offering formula from BM EA 558:

BM EA 558,
Lines 1-2:

ḥtp-di-nsw ꜣsir nb ḏdw nṯr ꜥꜣ nb ꜣbḏw
di=f prt-ḥrw t ḥnḳt kꜣ ꜣpd šs mnḫt ...
An offering which the king gives to Osiris lord of Djedu, great god, lord of Abydos,
so that he might give an invocation offering of bread, beer, ox and fowl, alabaster and linen ...

b. Causation

We have already noted the use of the verb *rdi* to express causation when followed by another verb with the sense of 'to cause/have/let/allow someone to do something' (see §40). This other verb goes in the future *sḏm(=f)* form:

Ikhernofret's description of the great procession of Osiris:

Berlin 1204,
Lines 18-19:
iw ir.n=i prt ꜥꜣt šms=i nṯr r nmtt=f di.n=i sḳd dpt-nṯr
I conducted the great procession, following the god at his travels, and I made the god's boat **sail**

§58 Negation

The future *sḏm(=f)* in its main usage is negated by ⌇ *nn* + **future sḏm(=f)**: 'you will/may not do that':

The bottom section of BM EA 101 is based on the goodwill and wish elements of the
appeal to the living (i.e. that good things will happen to passers-by when they say the
offering formula for the deceased):

BM EA 101,
Lines 2-4:

swḏ=ṯn iȝ(w)t=ṯn n ẖrd(w)=ṯn ... nn ḥḳr=ṯn nn ibi=ṯn
You will hand over your offices to your children ... you will not be
hungry, you will not be thirsty

§59 Forms of the *sḏmty.fy* and the future *sḏm(=f)*

The *sḏmty.fy* and the future *sḏm(=f)* have the following forms:
a. *sḏmty.fy*

	SINGULAR		PLURAL
	MASCULINE	FEMININE	
STRONG	sḏmty.fy	sḏmty.sy	sḏmty.sn
DOUBLING - doubling	mȝȝty.fy	mȝȝty.sy	mȝȝty.sn
WEAK	šdty.fy	šdty.sy	šdty.sn
EXTRA WEAK - *rdi* shows *r*	rdity.fy	rdity.sy	rdity.sn
iy(i)/iw(i) - shows *iw*	iwty.fy	iwty.sy	iwty.sn

b. *The future sḏm(=f):*

	FUTURE *sḏm(=f)*		
STRONG		sḏm=f	may he hear
DOUBLING - no doubling		mȝ=f	may he see
WEAK		mr=f or mry=f	may he love
EXTRA WEAK		di=f (no *r*)	may he give

SPECIAL CASES	⟨hieroglyphs⟩	*iwt=f* (with extra *-t*)	may he come
	⟨hieroglyphs⟩	*int=f* (with extra *-t*)	may he bring

Notes

i The verb *mꜣꜣ* 'to see' also displays a form ⟨hieroglyphs⟩ *mꜣn=f*.

ii The weak verb form with ⟨hieroglyphs⟩ *-y* is most common in the first person.

iii The forms from the verbs 'come' and 'bring' show an extra *t*.

§60 Adjectives in *-y*

When used with nouns, a special adjective form of the preposition is used:

The stela of Mentjuhotep:

Fitz.E9.1922,
Line 1:

⟨hieroglyphs⟩

*i ꜥnḫw **tpw** tꜣ ...*
O the living **(who are) upon** the earth ...

Here ⟨hieroglyphs⟩ *tpw* is an adjective derived from the preposition ⟨hieroglyphs⟩ *tp* ('upon'). As an adjective ⟨hieroglyphs⟩ *tpw* agrees with the noun ⟨hieroglyphs⟩ *ꜥnḫw* (both show the plural *-w*). This form is termed the *adjective in -y* (the *-y* only occurs in the masculine singular form). Some prepositions display a distinctive writing in the adjective in *-y*:

	PREPOSITION			ADJECTIVE IN *-y*	
⟨hieroglyph⟩	*m*	in	⟨hieroglyphs⟩	*imy*	(which/who is) in
⟨hieroglyph⟩	*r*	at, towards in relation to	⟨hieroglyphs⟩	*iry*	(which/who is) at, towards, relating to
⟨hieroglyph⟩	*ḥr*	upon	⟨hieroglyphs⟩	*ḥry*	(which/who is) upon
⟨hieroglyph⟩	*tp*	upon	⟨hieroglyphs⟩ or ⟨hieroglyphs⟩	*tpy*	(which/who is) upon

Adjectives in *-y* agree with their nouns in number and gender:

		ADJECTIVES IN *-y*				
	SG.	PL.			SG.	PL.
MSC.	⟨hiero⟩ *-y*	⟨hiero⟩ *-w*	e.g. MSC.		⟨hieroglyphs⟩ *imy*	⟨hieroglyphs⟩ *imw*
FEM.	⟨hiero⟩ *-t*	⟨hiero⟩ *-t*		FEM.	⟨hieroglyphs⟩ *imt*	⟨hieroglyphs⟩ *imt*

In writing, however, *-y* and *-w* are often omitted:

The stela of Inhuretnakht begins with an offering formula invoking Anubis:

BM EA 1783,
Line 1:

*ḥtp-di-nsw inpw **tp(y) ḏw=f im(y)** wt nb tꜣ ḏsr*
An offering which the king gives (to) Anubis who is **upon** his
mountain, **the one in** the *wt*-fetish, lord of the sacred land

Adjectives in *-y* are common in titles, for example:

	ḥry-sštꜣ	master of secrets (literally, the one upon secrets)		*ḥry-ḥbt*	lector priest (literally, the one carrying the lector book)

(*ḥry* is derived from the preposition *ḥr* 'under', which is also used with the sense of 'carrying'.)

Like other adjectives, the adjectives in *-y* can be used on their own ('the one who ...', 'the thing which ...'). A particular example is the name of Khentyimentu 'the foremost of the westerners':

The stela of Khuenbik begins with an offering formula invoking Osiris:

BM EA 584,
Line 1:

*ḥtp-di-nsw ꜣsir nb ḏdw **ḥnty-imntw** (nṯr) ꜥꜣ nb ꜣbḏw*
An offering which the king gives to Osiris lord of Djedu,
Khentyimentu, great (god), lord of Abydos

(*nṯr* has been omitted in the phrase *nṯr ꜥꜣ* 'great god')

ḥnty is an adjective in *-y* meaning '(the one) at the front'. *imntw* is also an adjective in *-y*, derived from the noun *imnt* 'the west' and means 'the ones of the west','westerners'. So *ḥnty-imntw* means 'the one at the front of the westerners' (the 'westerners' are the dead, the people in the realm of sunset).

VOCABULARY

	is	tomb		*mnw-nfr*	Minnefer
	mnṯw-ḥtp	Mentjuhotep		*msḏ(i)*	hate
	r-pr	temple		*ḥm(w)-nṯr*	*ḥm*-priests
	ḥm(w)t-nṯr	*ḥm*-priestesses		*ḥpt*	death
	sꜣḫ	transfigure			

Exercises

8.1 Signs

a. 2-consonant and 3-consonant signs:

b. Three other signs which are useful at this point:

SIGN		EXAMPLE	
⌐ or ◥	E30/E31 – combination of ◥ E29 and D32 (and C11 – sandy hill-slope)	⌐ or ◥	*ḥrt-nṯr*	necropolis, cemetery
〡	E17 – dagger. Used in the adjective in -*y tpy*	〡	*tpy*	(who is) upon. See §60 above
✛	E33 – two planks crossed and joined. Used in the adjective in -*y ỉmy*.		*ỉmy*	(who is) in. See §60 above

8.2 Words

Transliterate the following words:

.... receive, take		.... transfigure
.... tomb, cenotaph		.... entourage
.... tomb		.... akh-spirit

(The blessed dead become ꜣḫ-spirits in the afterlife by being transfigured (sꜣḫ) after death.)

8.3 BM EA 567

BM EA 567 (shown on p. 120) begins with a date, an offering formula, and then moves onto a full set of the twenty elements of the Abydos formula, of which a selection are given here, including some mentioning the Abydos mysteries. Ignore the sections in grey.

BM EA 567
(carved limestone; w. 63.5cm)

Notes

i See notes to Exercise 7.8 for the writing of the determinative of *ḏdw* and *ꜣbḏw*.

ii Wepwawet has the epithet *ḫnty ꜣbḏw* 'the one at the front/head of Abydos' (see §60 above for *ḫnty*).

iii The names of Heket and Khnum are written with their frog and ram determinatives respectively.

iv *ḫt -nbt nfr(t) pr(r)t m-bꜣḥ nṯr ꜥꜣ* 'everything good which goes before the great god'. *pr(r)t* is a participle.

v In Line 5 the Abydos formula begins with *ms.t(w) -n=f ꜥwy ḫr ...* 'May arms be presented to him carrying ...' The two groups of the venerated dead noted are *šmsw n ꜣsir* 'the followers of Osiris' and *tp-ꜥ ḫprw ḫr-ḥꜣt* 'the ancestors who existed before'.

vi In Line 5 *-ṯw* is the dependent pronoun 'you' (the owner Amenemhet is sometimes referred to as 'he' sometimes as 'you'). See §41.

vii On *šnyt im(yt) ꜣbḏw*, see §60.

viii In Line 8 *ḏ* in *ḏd* is flatter than the normal form. Notice that it does not have the horns of the *f*-viper.

ix Translate *nšmt wrt r nmtt=s* as 'when the great *nšmt*-bark is at its journeys'.

 x In Line 10 *t₃-wr*, the nome containing Abydos, here refers to the inhabitant of the nome, hence it can have a 'mouth'.

xi Insert 'at' in your translation before *h₃kr* in Line 10.

xii The vigil of Horus-*šn* or Horus the fighter remains one of the most elusive aspects of the Osiris mysteries, although it probably refers to part of the rites concerned with the reanimation of the dead Osiris.

When you have finished both Exercises 8.3 and 8.5, you may wish to compare the Abydos formulae on the two stelae.

VOCABULARY

𓅭	*iiw*	welcome	𓂝𓏭	*ꜥwy*	arms
𓅨	*wr(w)*	the great	𓅓𓐍	*m-bꜣḥ*	before
𓄟	*ms*	present, offer	𓂋𓊪𓈎	*r-pḳr*	Ro-Poker (Poker)
𓎛𓀁	*h₃kr*	Haker-rites	𓎛𓈖𓅱	*hnw*	jubilation
𓎛𓈖𓂝	*ḥnꜥ*	together with	𓊵𓏏𓊪	*ḥtp*	offerings, peace
𓑰𓏃	*ẖnty*	(the one) at the front	𓁷	*ẖr*	carrying, under
𓋴𓂧𓅓	*sdm < sḏm*	hear (the *ḏ* has changed into *d* over time)	𓋴𓆓𓂻	*sḏ₃*	travel
𓋴𓂧𓂋𓏏	*sḏrt*	vigil	�𓂻𓅭𓏭	*šmsw*	followers
𓈙𓈖𓏏	*šnyt*	entourage	𓎼𓂋𓎛	*grḥ*	night
𓇾𓅨	*t₃-wr*	Tawer (nome)	𓏏𓊪𓂝	*tp(w)-ꜥ*	ancestors

 sḏryt nt ḥr-šn   the vigil of Horus-*šn*

8.4 Study exercise: BM EA 584

Transliterate and translate the stela of Khuenbik (BM EA 584 shown on p. 122) with its appeal to the living.

Note

In Lines 4–5 *m mrr=ṯn šms wp-w₃wt r nmtt=f nb* 'in that you wish to follow Wepwawet at all his journeys'; *šms* is in the infinitive form and supplies the object of the wish.

BM EA 584
(carved limestone; H. 53cm)

VOCABULARY

	m ḫsft	in going south		*m ḫd*	in going north
or	*m-r iḳdw*	overseer of builders		*mꜥḥꜥt*	cenotaph, tomb
	mꜣi-n-ḥr	Maienhor (name)		*ptḥ-ḥtp*	Ptahhotep (name)
	n-ptḥ-kꜣw	Niptahkau (name)		*nmtt*	journeys

VOCABULARY   (CONTINUED)

	rn	name		*rrwt*	Rerut (name)
	ḥkt	(the goddess) Heket		*ḥtp*	offerings
	ḫw-n-bik	Khuenbik (name)		*ḫnmw*	(the god) Khnum
	sꜥnḫ	make live, perpetuate		*smyt imntt*	the western desert
	šms	to follow		*df(ꜣw)*	provisions

8.5 Study exercise: BM EA 162

The final stela for you to study is BM EA 162, the stela of the general-in-chief Ameny. The stela is shown on p. 125. As usual, transliterate and translate with the help of the accompanying vocabulary.

Notes

  i See Exercise 3.3 for vocabulary for the offering formula section.

  ii Read *di.t(w)* at the beginning of Line 4 with ▭ for ▭.

  iii See Chapter 7 for the structure of the various epithets.

VOCABULARY

or	*i(i)w*	welcome	or	*ꜥwy*	arms
or	*wr(w)*	the great		*ḥb(w)*	festivals
	ḥtp	peace, satisfaction		*ḥtpt*	offerings
	ḥtp ꜥꜣ	great altar		*šsp*	receive

FESTIVALS

	wꜣg	Wag-festival		*prt mnw*	procession of Min
	ḏḥwtt	Thoth-festival		*prt spdt*	procession of Sothis
	ḥb skr	Soker-festival		*tp-rnpt*	beginning of the lunar year

TITLES AND OCCUPATIONS

	ḥm-nṯr ḥwt-ḥr	priestess of Hathor		*m-r ḫtmt*	overseer of the treasury
	ḥm-kꜣ	ka-priest		*m-r mšꜥ wr*	general-in-chief

TITLES AND OCCUPATIONS   (CONTINUED)

	wbȝt	cup-bearer			*nšt*	hairdresser
	ḥry-pr	domestic servant				

NAMES

	imny	Ameny
	ḫwyt	Khuyet
	ḫnt-ḫty-ḥtp	Khenetkhetyhetep
	sȝ-ḥwt-ḥr	Sahathor
	sȝt-sbk	Satsobek
	mdḥw	Medhu
	sȝ-ḫnt-ḫty	Sakhenetkhety
	sȝwtyt	Sautyt
	sȝt-ḫnt-ḫti	Satkhenetkhety
	ḏfȝ-ḥˁp(y)	Djefahapy

Once you have read this stela, it will no doubt strike you that the owner himself is actually missing from the figures shown. This is because, like a number of stelae from Abydos, BM EA 162 belongs to a group dedicated in an offering-chapel at the site. Unfortunately, Abydos was cleared of many of its Middle Kingdom monuments by collectors and early archaeologists in the nineteenth century without a proper record being made of the find-sites. It is only through the work of scholars scouring the museum collections of the world and sifting through the sparse archaeological record that original groups of stelae are gradually being reassembled.

Fortunately, BM EA 162 has been allocated to a group now known conventionally as Abydos North Offering Chapel (ANOC) 2. It has a companion, now in the Egyptian Museum, Cairo (CCG 20546), which shows the same style and phraseology: the two were clearly made in the same workshop as a pair. It too lacks a figure of Ameny himself; instead it depicts further relatives and dependants looking from left to right (whereas in BM EA 162 they look from right to left). This pair of stelae no doubt framed a central stela depicting Ameny himself; one piece which has been proposed is in the Musée du Louvre, Paris (C35).

BM EA 162
(carved limestone; H. 113cm)

About the Front Cover

The cover shows a detail of an inscribed ritual tool used in the rite of 'opening the mouth' – an obscure ceremony designed to breathe life into an embalmed corpse, a statue or an inscribed image. The text records a dedication from Senwosret I to his celebrated predecessor (here termed *it* '(fore)father'), Mentjuhotep II of the 11th Dynasty, who is here identified by his praenomen Nebhepetre.

MMA 24.21:

ntr nfr nb tꜣwy s-n-wsrt
ir.n=f m mnw=f n it=f nb-ḥpt-rꜥ mꜣꜥ-ḥrw

The perfect god, the lord of the twin lands, Senwosret:
he has made a dedication for his father,
Nebhepetre, the justified.

mnw 'dedication' refers here to the opening of the mouth implement itself and the rites associated with it. *mnw* is often translated as 'monument' in dictionaries, but actually refers more generally to royal dedications, here for a celebrated royal predecessor.

The appearance of an extra *m* before the object *mnw* is a standard part of this dedication formula, although the reason for it is still disputed by scholars (as indeed are the intricacies of the grammar of the formula) – so you certainly should not worry too much about it. According to one suggestion, it indicates that it is the dedication of the object itself which is seen as the focal-point of the formula, focusing on Senwosret's performance of the commemorative functions of kingship through supplying the opening of the mouth implement for the animation of statues of his celebrated predecessor.

VOCABULARY

| | *mnw* | dedication | | *nb-ḥpt-rꜥ* | Nebhepetre |

Hieroglyphic sign-lists for the exercises

The following lists are intended to help you to identify particular hiero-glyphs quickly and easily, and then work out how they have been used to write words. You can also, if you wish, treat them as a convenient resource for memorising some of the most commonly used hieroglyphs.

List I: 1-consonant signs

ꜣ		Called *aleph*. Originally a throaty trill, it later became a stop, as in cockney pronunciation of *bottle* as *bo'l*, and *a hat* as *a 'a'*
i		Called *yodh*. Originally a stop, it tended to sound more like *y*. A weak sound, often not written
y	¹ ²	Like *y* in *yes*
ꜥ		Called *ayin*. A throaty gurgle, like saying *a* whilst swallowing
w	¹ ²	Called *waw*. Like *w* in *wet*. A weak sound, often not written
b		Like *b* in *bet*
p		Like *p* in *pet*
f		Like *f* in *fit*
m		Like *m* in *met*
n		Like *n* in *net*
r		Like *r* in *rain*, but distinctly trilled as in Scots pronunciation
h		Like *h* in *home*
ḥ		Emphatic *h* pronounced in the throat
ḫ		Like Scots *ch* in *loch*
ẖ		Slightly softer than *ḫ*, like German *ch* in *ich*
s	¹ ²	Like *s* in *soap*
š		Like *sh* in *ship*
ḳ		*k* pronounced at back of mouth, like Arabic *q* in *Qurꜥân* (Koran)
k		Like *k* in *kit*
g		Like *g* in *get*
t		Like *t* in *tub*
ṯ		Like *t* in *tune*
d		Like *d* in *did*
ḏ		Like *j* in *joke*, or French *di* in *dieu*

List II: Some common 2-consonant signs

	ꜣw		bꜣ		nb		ḫt		ḳd
	ꜣb or mr		bḥ or ḥw		nm		ḥꜣ		kꜣ
	ꜣḫ		pꜣ		nn		ḫn		km
	iw		pr		nḫ		ḥn		gm
	in or nw		pḥ		ns		ḥr		gs
	ir		mꜣ		nḏ		sꜣ		tꜣ
	is		mi		hꜣ		sꜣ		ti
	or ꜥꜣ		mw		ḥw or bḥ		sꜣ		tp
	ꜥḳ		mn		ḥm		sw		tm
	ꜥḏ		mr		ḥn		sn		ṯꜣ
	wꜣ		mr		ḥr		sk or wꜣḥ		ḏꜣ
	wꜥ		mr or ꜣb		ḥs		šꜣ		ḏw
	wp		mḥ		ḥḏ		šw		ḏr
	wn		ms		ḫꜣ		šn		ḏd
	wr		mt		ḫꜥ		šs		
	wḏ		m(w)t		ḫw		šd		

List III: Some common 3-consonant signs

	iꜣm or imꜣ		wꜣḥ or sk		mꜣꜥ		ḥꜣt		ḫnt		sšm
	iwn		wꜥb		nbw		ḥkꜣ		ḫrw		šps
	ꜥnḫ		wḥm		nfr		ḥtp		ḫnm		šms
	ꜥḥꜥ		wsr		nṯr		ḫpr		spd		dwꜣ

List IV: Some common ideograms

	=i	I, my (§36)		iwn	pillar		ꜥḥ	palace
	iꜣt	office		ib	heart		ꜥḥꜣ	fight
	iꜣw	praise		imnt	west		wꜣt	road, way
	ii	come		ꜥ	arm		wꜥb	pure

	pr	house, estate		*rnpt*	year		*sr*	official
	mšꜥ	expedition		*rd(i)*	give		*sḫt*	countryside
	n	not (§39)		*rdwy*	legs		*sḏm*	hear
	nwt	town		*ḥꜣt*	front		*špsy*	dignified
	nmtt	step, journey		*ḥr*	(1) face (2) on		*kꜣ*	ox, bull
	nṯr	god		*ḥtp*	offering		*t*	bread
	nḏm	sweet		*st*	seat, place		*tꜣ*	land
	r	mouth		*spꜣt*	district		*tp*	upon
	rꜥ	sun		*smsw*	elder, eldest		*ḏsr*	(1) clear (2) sacred

List V: Full Sign List

What follows is a complete list of signs appearing in this book, with an explanation of the different ways in which each one has been used to write words.
Since this is a practical list designed to help you find an unfamiliar sign
quickly, more recognisable signs have been grouped into three broad categories (humans, animals, nature), whilst others have been grouped by shape
(small, tall, broad). The signs are given here in a standardised font, but it
should be remembered that there will be some variation in their forms as
they appear on monuments; in particular, the details of a sign will be
affected by whether it is painted (as on a coffin) or inscribed (as on a stela).

Readers who continue their study of ancient Egyptian will eventually
need to become familiar with the systematic sign-list of Gardiner's *Egyptian
Grammar* (see p. 176). Since Gardiner used many more categories than we
have, there is no correspondence between his list and ours in the way a particular sign is classified. Here, we have used the following abbreviations: 1c.,
one-consonant sign; 2c., two-consonant sign; 3c., three-consonant sign;
ideo., ideogram; com., sign combined with other elements.

Index

§A. Signs depicting people or parts of the human body

A1	A2	A3	A4	A5	A6	A7	A8	A9	A10	A11	A12

| A13 | A14 | A15 | A16 | A17 | A18 | A19 | A20 | A21 | A22 | A23 | A24 |

| A25 | A26 | A27 | A28 | A29 | A30 | A31 | A32 | A33 | A34 | A35 | A36 |

| A37 | A38 | A39 | A40 | A41 | A42 | A43 | A44 | A45 | A46 | A47 | A48 |

| A49 | A50 | A51 | A52 | A53 | A54 | A55 | A56 | A57 | A58 | A59 | A60 |

| A61 | A62 |

§B. Signs depicting creatures or parts of their bodies

| B1 | B2 | B3 | B4 | B5 | B6 | B7 | B8 | B9 | B10 | B11 | B12 |

| B13 | B14 | B15 | B16 | B17 | B18 | B19 | B20 | B21 | B22 | B23 | B24 |

| B25 | B26 | B27 | B28 | B29 | B30 | B31 | B32 | B33 | B34 | B35 | B36 |

| B37 | B38 | B39 | B40 | B41 | B42 | B43 | B44 | B45 | B46 | B47 | B48 |

| B49 | B50 | B51 | B52 | B53 | B54 | B55 | B56 | B57 | B58 | B59 | B60 |

| B61 | B62 | B63 | B64 | B65 | B66 | B67 |

§C. Signs involving sky, earth, water, or plants

| C1 | C2 | C3 | C4 | C5 | C6 | C7 | C8 | C9 | C10 | C11 | C12 |

| C13 | C14 | C15 | C16 | C17 | C18 | C19 | C20 | C21 | C22 | C23 | C24 |

| C25 | C26 | C27 | C28 | C29 | C30 | C31 | C32 | C33 |

§D. Other small signs

D1	D2	D3	D4	D5	D6	D7	D8	D9	D10	D11	D12

D13	D14	D15	D16	D17	D18	D19	D20	D21	D22	D23	D24

D25	D26	D27	D28	D29	D30	D31	D32	D33	D34	D35	D36

D37	B45

§E. Other tall signs

E1	E2	E3	B54	E4	E5	E6	E7	E8	E9	E10	E11

E12	E13	E14	E15	E16	E17	E18	E19	E20	E21	E22	E23

E24	E25	E26	E27	E28	E29	E30	E31	E32	E33	E34	E35

E36	E37	E38	E39	E40	E41	E42	E43	E44	E45	E46	E47

E48	E49	E50	E51	E52	E53	E54	E55	E56	E57	E58	E59

E60	E61	E62	E63	E64	E65	E66	E67	E68	E69	E70	E71

§F. Other broad signs

F1	F2	F3	F4	F5	F6	F7	F8	F9	F10	F11	F12

F13	F14	F15	F16	F17	F18	F19	F20	F21	F22	F23	F24

F25	F26	F27	F28	F29	F30	F31	F32	F33	F34	F35	F36

F37	F38	F39	F40	F41	F42	F43	F44	F45	F46	F47	F48

F49	F50	F51	F52	F53	F54	F55	F56	F57

Full list

§A. Signs depicting people or parts of the human body

A1	man seated	(1) det. man, occupations of men; (2) ideo. or det. 'I, me, my' (§36, §41, §49)
A2	woman seated	det. woman, occupations of women
A3	god seated	det. god, names/titles of gods
A4	goddess with feather on head	ideo. or det. *mꜣꜥt* 'harmony', especially if personified as a goddess (compare with B27)
A5	man seated with hand to mouth	det. eat, speak, emotion (§6)
A6	man kneeling in adoration	det. *hnw* 'jubilation'
A7	official with staff and leather grip	(1) ideo. *sr* 'official'; (2) hence det. official
A8	man leaning on forked stick	ideo. *smsw* 'elder, eldest'
A9	old man leaning on stick	det. or abb. *iꜣw* 'old'
A10	official holding flail	(1) ideo. *špsy* 'dignified' and related words; (2) det. deceased official
A11	official seated	alternative form of A10
A12	man striking two-handed with staff	det. effort, action, violence
A13	man striking	ideo. or det. *ḥwi* 'strike'
A14	man building wall	(1) det. build; (2) abb. *iḳd* 'builder'
A15	man falling	det. fall, fell, overthrow
A16	man falling with blood streaming	det. enemy
A17	man gesturing	det. *i* the interjection 'O!'
A18	man standing with hand to mouth	det. *srḫ* 'talk about, accuse'
A19	man with arms raised in joy	det. rejoice
A20	man with arms in adoration	(1) abb. *dwꜣ* 'adore'; (2) hence det. adore
A21	man slumped	det. tired, weak

A22		woman giving birth	det. give birth
A23		infant	(1) det. child; (2) hence abb. *ḫrd* 'child'; (3) 2c. *nn* (or *nni*)
A24		soldier	ideo. or det. *mšꜥ* 'expedition, army'
A25		man seated with dagger	ideo. or det. *iry* 'keeper'
A26		royal figure with flail	(1) variant of A27; (2) det. *ḫnty-imntw* (a name of the god Osiris)
A27		royal figure	(1) abb. *nsw* 'king'; (2) det. names of the god Osiris
A28		figure of Amun	ideo. *imn* '(the god) Amun'
A29		priest com. water pouring from jug	(1) alternative for A55; (2) hence ideo. *wꜥb* 'priest'
A30		mummy on bier	det. lying down, death
A31		face	(1) ideo. *ḥr* 'face', 'on'; (2) hence 2c. *ḥr*
A32		head in profile	(1) ideo. *tp* 'head', 'upon'; (2) hence 2c. *tp*
A33		hair	det. hair
A34		front of face	det. face, nose, e.g. *sn* 'kiss'
A35		eyes com. falcon markings	ideo. *ptr* 'observe, view'
A36		eye	(1) 2c. *ir*; (2) det. *mꜣꜣ* 'see'
A37		eye with cosmetic	det. actions or conditions of the eye
A38		mouth	(1) ideo. *r* 'mouth'; (2) hence 1c. *r*
A39		hand	1c. *d*
A40		arm	(1) ideo. *ꜥ* 'arm'; (2) hence 1c. *ꜥ*; (3) often alternative for A41–44
A41		arm offering loaf (E61)	(1) ideo. *di* or *rdi* 'give', alternative for E61; (2) read *m* or *mi* in the names *bꜣ-mkt* and *dwꜣ-mwt=f* by confusion with another sign
A42		arm holding stick	det. action, violence, effort, alternative for A12
A43		arm holding flail	2c. *ḫw*
A44		arm holding wand or lettuce	ideo. *ḏsr* 'sacred' and related words
A45		arms holding shield and axe	ideo. *ꜥḥꜣ* 'fight' and related words
A46		arms rowing	2c. *ẖn*
A47		arms gesturing denial	ideo. the negative words *n* (§39) and *nn* (§58)
A48		arms raised	(1) ideo. *kꜣ* 'ka'; (2) hence 2c. *kꜣ*
A49		arms com. E3	abb. *ḥm-kꜣ* 'ka-priest'

A50		boat's mast (E56) com. A40	3c. ꜥḥꜥ, alternative for E56
A51		breast	det. breast, suckle
A52		penis	(1) det. male; (2) 2c. *mt*
A53		penis with issue of fluid	det. or abb. *bꜣḥ* in *m-bꜣḥ* 'in the presence of'
A54		lower leg	1c. *b*
A55		A54 com. water pouring from jug	ideo. or det. *wꜥb* 'pure' and related words
A56		leg	(1) ideo. or det. *rd* 'leg'; (2) det. tread
A57		legs walking	(1) det. motion; (2) ideo. *iw(i)* 'come'; (3) ideo. *nmtt* '(formal) journey'
A58		C20 com. A57	combined sound-sign and det. for *i(i)* 'come'
A59		D33 com. A57	combined sound-sign and det. for *in(i)* 'bring'
A60		F15 com. A57	combined sound-sign and det. for words suggesting motion which include the sound *s*, e.g. *sb(i)* 'go', *ms* 'bring'
A61		F29 com. A57	combined sound-sign and det. for *sšm* 'conduct' and related words, alternative for F29
A62		F33 com. A57	combined sound-sign and det. for *iṯ(i)* 'seize'

§B. Signs depicting creatures or parts of their bodies.

B1		quail chick	1c. *w*
B2		owl	1c. *m*
B3		Egyptian vulture	1c. *ꜣ*
B4		pair of vultures	variant of B3 when writing *ꜣꜣ*
B5		buzzard	2c. *tw*, especially at the end of words, often confused with B3
B6		guinea-fowl	2c. *nḥ*
B7		pintail duck	(1) 2c. *sꜣ*; (2) det. bird, alternative for B8
B8		white-fronted goose	(1) 2c. *gb*; (2) det. bird
B9		duck in flight	2c. *pꜣ*
B10		trussed goose or duck	det. goose
B11		head of duck	abb. *ꜣpd* 'bird'
B12		duckling	2c. *ṯꜣ*
B13		pair of plovers	ideo. or det. *rḥty* 'washerman'

B14		cormorant	2c. ʿk
B15		jabiru	2c. bꜣ
B16		human-headed bird com. bowl	ideo. bꜣ 'soul' (New Kingdom)
B17		falcon	(1) det. falcon; (2) hence ideo. ḥr '(the god) Horus'
B18		B17 com. E52	ideo. ḥwt-ḥr '(the goddess) Hathor'
B19		falcon perched	det. gods
B20		falcon-headed god	ideo. rʿ '(the god) Re'
B21		sparrow	det. small, weak, pathetic
B22		swallow	2c. wr
B23		vulture	(1) ideo. mwt 'mother'; (2) hence 2c. mt
B24		black ibis	(1) ideo. gm 'find'; (2) hence 2c. gm
B25		crested ibis	2c. ꜣḫ in ꜣḫ 'akh-spirit' and related words
B26		sacred ibis	ideo. ḏḥwty '(the god) Thoth'
B27		feather	(1) 2c. šw; (2) abb. mꜣʿt 'harmony'
B28		egg	ideo. or det. ꜣst '(the goddess) Isis'
B29		ox	ideo. or det. ox, bull, cattle
B30		head of ox	abb. kꜣ 'ox'
B31		calf	det. cattle
B32		new-born calf	2c. iw
B33		kid	2c. ib
B34		ram	det. ram, sheep
B35		B34 com. bowl	abb. bꜣ 'ram'
B36		hide of goat	2c. ẖn
B37		hide pierced by arrow	det. pierce
B38		piece of flesh	(1) det. flesh; (2) ideo. ꜣst '(the goddess) Isis'
B39		foreleg of ox	ideo. or det. ḫpš 'foreleg' (of animal), 'strong arm' (of man)
B40		leg of ox	3c. wḥm
B41		animal belly with tail	1c. ẖ
B42		ox horns	2c. wp
B43		ox ear	ideo. or det. sḏm 'hear'

B44		ox tongue	(1) ideo. *m-r* 'overseer' (§24b); (2) 2c. *ns*
B45		heart	ideo. or det. *ib* 'heart'
B46		spine with issue of marrow	det. or abb. *imꜣḫ* 'veneration' and related words
B47		spine with issue of marrow at ends	2c. *ꜣw*
B48		head of leopard	ideo. or det. *pḥty* 'strength'
B49		forepart of lion	(1) ideo. *ḥꜣt* 'front'; (2) hence 3c. *ḥꜣt*
B50		hindpart of lion	2c. *pḥ*
B51		desert dog	det. dog, including the god Wepwawet
B52		dog com. standard	ideo. or det. *wp-wꜣwt* '(the god) Wepwawet'
B53		dog com. shrine	ideo. or det. *inpw* '(the god) Anubis'
B54		head of dog	3c. *wsr*
B55		god with head of mythical animal	ideo. *sty* '(the god) Seth'
B56		hare	2c. *wn*
B57		pair of crocodiles	ideo. *ity* 'sovereign'
B58		mummified crocodile	ideo. *sbk* '(the god) Sobek'
B59		crocodile on shrine	ideo. *sbk* '(the god) Sobek', alternative for B58
B60		cobra	1c. *ḏ*
B61		horned viper	(1) 1c. *f*; (2) det.(?) *it* 'father'
B62		E16 com. B61	3c. *ḥsf*, alternative for E16
B63		frog	det. frog, including the goddess Heket
B64		fish	det. or abb. fish
B65		oxyrhynchus fish	2c. *ḫꜣ*
B66		dung beetle	3c. *ḫpr*
B67		bee	abb. *bity* 'king'

§C. Signs depicting sky, earth, water or plants

C1	⊙	sun-disc	(1) det. sun, day, time; (2) ideo. *rꜥ* 'sun', '(the god) Re'
C2		sunrise above hills	2c. *ḥꜥ*
C3		canopy of the sky	(1) det. sky; (2) det. *ḥry* 'which is upon' (§60)
C4		C3 com. E3	det. night, darkness

C5		crescent moon	(1) det. moon, event based on lunar month; (2) ideo. *iꜥḥ* 'moon'
C6		star	(1) in *dwꜣ* 'adore'; (2) det. star; (3) det. *wnwt* 'priesthood'
C7		C5 com. C6	ideo. *ꜣbd* 'month' and related words
C8		half moon com. C6	ideo. half-month festival, reading uncertain (see p. 76)
C9		strip of land com. D4	(1) 2c. *tꜣ*; (2) det. in *ḏt* 'eternity'
C10		strip of land	alternative form of C9
C11		slope of hill	1c. *ḳ*
C12		valley between hills	2c. *ḏw*
C13		desert hills	(1) det. desert; (2) ideo. *ḫꜣst* 'foreign land'
C14		terraced slope	det. terrace
C15		ripple of water	1c. *n*
C16		group of ripples	(1) det. water, cleanse; (2) 2c. *mw*
C17		garden pool	1c. *š*
C18		pool with flowers	2c. *šꜣ*
C19		reeds	ideo. or det. *sḫt* 'countryside'
C20		reed	1c. *i*
C21		pair of reeds	1c. *y*
C22		herb	(1) det. plant; (2) 2c. *ḥn*
C23		lotus	(1) 2c. *ḫꜣ*; (2) abb. *ḫꜣ* 'thousand', or units per thousand in counting
C24		clump of papyrus	2c. *ḥꜣ*
C25		sedge plant	(1) 2c. *sw*; (2) abb. *nsw* 'king'
C26		C25 com. D16	abb. *rḫ-nsw* 'king's adviser'
C27		flowering sedge	ideo. or det. *šmꜥ* 'Upper Egypt'
C28		pair of rushes	2c. *nn*
C29		tree	(1) det. tree; (2) 3c. *iꜣm, imꜣ*
C30		tree branch	(1) det. *ḫt* 'wood' and related words; (2) hence 2c. *ḫt* ; (3) det. *pḳr* 'Poker', and *ḥꜣkr* 'Haker-rites'
C31		scented pod	(1) ideo. or det. *nḏm* 'sweet'; (2) hence 3c. *nḏm*
C32		scented rhysome	ideo. or det. *bnr* 'sweet'
C33		thorn	(1) ideo. or det. *spd* 'sharp, keen'; (2) hence 3c. *spd*

§D. Other small signs

D1			single stroke	(1) indicates word group or ideogram (§13); (2) abb. *wꜥ* 'one', or units of one in counting (§19)
D2	\\	pair of strokes	1c. *y*, especially as the dual ending (§15)
D3	ǀ ǀ ǀ	three strokes	(1) det. plurals (§8); (2) det. singular nouns which represent collections of individuals, e.g. 𓈘 *mšꜥ* 'expedition'
D4	ₒₒₒ	grains of sand	det. mineral
D5	∩	cattle hobble	abb. *mḏw* 'ten', or units of ten in counting (§19)
D6	⊐⊏	irrigation canals	det. irrigated land
D7	×	crossed sticks	det. separate, cross, pass by
D8	◿	burning charcoal with flames	(1) ideo. *km* 'black'; (2) hence 2c. *km*
D9	⌷	reed shelter	1c. *h*
D10	℮	B1 as abbreviated for hieratic	1c. *w*, alternative for B1
D11	?	coil of rope	(1) det. rope; (2) abb. *š(n)t* 'hundred', or units per hundred in counting
D12	ঢ়	twisted cord	(1) 2c. *šs*; (2) hence abb. *šs* 'alabaster'
D13	ঢ়	twisted cord	2c. *šn*
D14	ঢ়	twisted cord (?)	det. *ḥbsw* 'clothing'
D15	☐	reed mat or stool	1c. *p*
D16	⊜	placenta (?), ball of string (?)	1c. *ḫ*
D17	◎	threshing-floor	2c. *sp*
D18	⊗	roads within enclosure	(1) ideo. *nwt* 'town'; (2) hence det. town, estate
D19	⊙	round loaf	det. *pꜣt* 'beginning of time', from a word *pꜣt* 'loaf' (similar writing)
D20	⊖	moon partly obscured	(1) 3c. *psḏ*; (2) by confusion, alternative for D19
D21	◌	pustule	(1) det. *wt* in *imy-wt*, title of Anubis; (2) det. scent, odour, disease; (3) abb. *ḥsb* 'count' and related words
D22	◌	pustule with issue of fluid	det. scent, odour, disease, alternative for D21
D23	◡	log stripped of bark	det. scent, scented wood
D24	◠	bun	(1) 1c. *t*; (2) abb. *it* in *it-nṯr* 'god's father'
D25	θ	small loaf	det. or abb. *t* 'bread'
D26	⌸	kiln	2c. *tꜣ*

D27	𓏗	beer jug	det. or abb. *ḥnḳt* 'beer'
D28	𓏘	basin (?)	det. *šnꜥw* 'magazine'
D29	𓏙	well full of water	2c. *ḥm*
D30	𓏚	bundle of flax	2c. *ḏr*
D31	𓏛	jar-stand	(1) 1c. *g*; (2) ideo. *nst* 'throne'
D32	𓏜	butcher's block	2c. *ḫr*
D33	𓏝	pot	(1) 2c. *nw*; (2) 2c. *in* (§49); (3) often as a graphic complement for *nḏ* (E15) and *ḳd* (E24).
D34	𓏞	three pots	(1) 2c. *nw*, alternative for D33 at the end of a word; (2) 3c. *nnw* (?) in the name *nnwy*
D35	𓏟	stone jug	3c. *ḫnm*
D36	𓏠	part of steering-gear of boat (?)	(1) ideo. *ḥpt* 'steering oar'; (2) hence 2c. *ḥp*
D37	𓏡	seal on necklace	ideo. or det. *ḫtm* 'seal' and related words
*	𓏢	heart	see B45

§E. Other tall signs

E1	𓏤	wooden staff	det. *ꜣryt* 'staff'
E2	𓏥	throw-stick	(1) det. throw; (2) det. foreigner, enemy; (3) det. *ḳmꜣ* 'create'
E3	𓏦	fuller's club	2c. *ḥm*
*	𓏧	head of dog	see B54
E4	𓏨	sceptre	3c. *wꜣs*
E5	𓏩	sceptre with feather	ideo. *wꜣst* 'Thebes'
E6	𓏪	sceptre with spiral shaft	3c. *ḏꜥm*
E7	𓏫	standard with feather	ideo. *imnt* 'the west' and related words
E8	𓏬	totem	ideo. or det. *mnw* '(the god) Min'
E9	𓏭	totem	ideo. *tꜣ-wr* 'the nome of Tawer'
E10	𓏮	totem	ideo. or det. *iꜣt* 'office'
E11	𓏯	crook	(1) ideo. *ḥḳꜣ* 'ruler'; (2) hence 3c. *ḥḳꜣ*
E12	𓏰	crook with package	ideo. *šms* 'follow' and related words
E13	𓏱	sceptre	(1) ideo. *ḫrp* 'control' and related words; (2) ideo. *sḫm* 'control' and related words
E14	𓏲	stone mace	2c. *ḥḏ*

E15		unknown	2c. *nḏ*, usually accompanied by D33
E16		spindle	3c. *ḫsf*
E17		archaic dagger	in *tpy* 'which is upon' (§60)
E18		butcher's knife	2c. *nm*
E19		butcher's knife	alternative for E18
E20		arrow head	2c. *sn*
E21		target pierced by arrows	det. *st(i)* or *st(i)* 'spear'
E22		cord wound on stick	2c. *wḏ*
E23		cord wound on stick	alternative for E22
E24		mortar float (?)	(1) ideo. or det. *ḳd* 'build' and related words; (2) hence 2c. *ḳd,* usually accompanied by D33
E25		notched palm	3c. *rnp*
E26		E25 com. D24	abb. *rnpt* 'year'
E27		pestle	2c. *ti*
E28		folded cloth	1c. *s*
E29		pennant	(1) ideo. *nṯr* 'god'; (2) hence 3c. *nṯr* in *snṯr* 'incense'
E30		E29 com. D32	ideo. *ẖrt-nṯr* 'cemetery'
E31		E29 com. C11 and D32	ideo. *ẖrt-nṯr* 'cemetery', alternative for E30
E32		three fox-skins	(1) 2c. *ms*; (2) a similar sign in *ȝbt* 'family, household' is probably a writing of E71
E33		crossed planks	in *imy* 'which is in' (§60)
E34		sandal strap	3c. *ꜥnḫ*
E35		twisted wick	1c. *ḥ*
E36		fibre swab	(1) 2c. *sk*; (2) 3c. *wȝḫ*
E37		water pot	2c. *ḥs*
E38		rack of water pots	3c. *ḫnt*
E39		rack of water pots	alternative for E38
E40		water pot with issue of contents	ideo. or det. *ḳbḥw* 'libation water' and related words
E41		water pot in stand	alternative for E40
E42		ointment jar	det. or abb. *mrḥt* 'ointment'
E43		ointment jar	alternative for E42
E44		chisel	(1) 2c. *ȝb*; (2) 2c. *mr*

E45		fire-drill	2c. *ḏꜣ*
E46		drill cutting bead	3c. *wbꜣ*, with a simpler variant
E47		palace facade	ideo. *ꜥḥ* 'palace'
E48		reed column	2c. *ḏd*
E49		wooden column	2c. *ꜥꜣ*
E50		pillar	(1) ideo. *iwn* 'pillar'; (2) hence 3c. *iwn*; (3) abb. *iwnw* 'the city of Heliopolis'
E51		shrine	ideo. or det. *sḥ* 'shrine'
E52		plan of estate	ideo. *ḥwt* 'enclosure, foundation'
E53		E52 com. D24 and F5	ideo. *nbt-ḥwt* '(the goddess) Nephthys'
E54		grain heap	ideo. or det. *šnwt* 'granary'
E55		fringed cloth	det. or abb. *mnḫt* 'linen'
E56		boat's mast	3c. *ꜥḥꜥ*
E57		oar	3c. *ḫrw*
E58		ship's sail	ideo. *ṯꜣw* 'breath'
E59		heart and windpipe	3c. *nfr*
E60		seat	(1) ideo. *st* 'place, seat'; (2) hence 2c. *st* ; (3) hence (?) 2c. *ꜣs(t)* in *ꜣsir* '(the god) Osiris' and *ꜣst* '(the goddess) Isis'
E61		offering loaf	ideo. *di* or *rdi* 'give', alternative for A41
E62		milk-jug within net	2c. *mi*
E63		lasso	2c. *wꜣ*
E64		brazier with flame	det. heat, cook
E65		bundle of reeds	2c. *is*
E66		pieces of wood lashed together	2c. *rs*
E67		stylised balance	alternative for E66
E68		wall ornament	ideo. or det. *ḫkrt* 'diadem, ornament'
E69		writing equipment	ideo. *sḫ* 'scribe'
E70		royal crown	1c. *n* (from the 13th dynasty onwards)
E71		faience necklace	det. (?) *ꜣbt* 'family, household', alternative for F8

§F. Other broad signs

F1		papyrus roll	det. write, abstractions (§6)
F2		papyrus roll	earlier form of F1
F3		papyrus roll	alternative form for F1
F4		basket with handle	1c. *k*
F5		basket	2c. *nb*
F6		basin com. canopy	(1) det. festival; (2) abb. *ḥb* 'festival'
F7		alabaster basin	alternative for F6
F8		stylised bowl	(1) det. *ꜣbw* 'the town of Elephantine'; (2) hence det. *ꜣbt* 'family, household' (similar writing)
F9		loaf (for offering)	det. bread, offerings
F10		loaf (for offering)	alternative form of F9
F11		loaf on mat	ideo. *ḥtp* 'offer' and related words
F12		plan of house	(1) ideo. *pr* 'house, estate'; (2) hence 2c. *pr*; (3) det. building, location
F13		F12 com. D25, D27 and E57	abb. *prt-ḫrw* 'voice offering'
F14		laden offering table	det. *dbḥt-ḥtp* 'ritual offerings'
F15		door bolt	1c. *s*
F16		wooden column	alternative form of E49
F17		fence	3c. *šsp*
F18		lid or door	det. open
F19		stone block (?)	det. *ḳrs* 'bury', perhaps as alternative for F18
F20		coffin	det. coffin, burial
F21		carrying chair	ideo. *ꜣsir* '(the god) Osiris' (see p. 41)
F22		statue plinth	3c. *mꜣꜥ*
F23		F22 com. F24	3c. *mꜣꜥ*
F24		sickle	2c. *mꜣ*
F25		hoe	2c. *mr*
F26		plough	(1) 3c. *šnꜥ*; (2) 2c. *hb*
F27		adze on block	3c. *stp*
F28		knife or saw	ideo. or det. *sfṯw* or *sfṯw* 'butcher'
F29		knife-sharpener	3c. *sšm*

F30	harpoon	2c. *wꜥ*
F31	whip	2c. *mḥ*
F32	water-skin	2c. *šd*
F33	tethering rope	1c. *ṯ*
F34	fringed cloth com. E28	det. clothing
F35	weaver's comb (?)	alternative form of F34
F36	netting needle	2c. *ꜥḏ*
F37	girdle knot	(1) ideo. *ṯs(i)* 'tie' and related words; (2) hence 2c. *ṯs*
F38	pair of ribs (?)	(1) 2c. *gs*; (2) sound complement for *im* or *m*
F39	vertebrae (?)	2c. *sꜣ*
F40	vertebrae (?)	later alternative for F39
F41	cattle hobble	2c. *sꜣ*
F42	road bordered by shrubs	ideo. or det. *wꜣt* 'road'
F43	canal	(1) 2c. *mr*, but read *m* in *mꜥḥꜥt* 'cenotaph'; (2) det. water
F44	irrigation canals	ideo. or det. *spꜣt* 'district'
F45	papyrus boat	det. papyrus boat
F46	papyrus (?) boat	det. *ḏꜣ(i)* 'ferry'
F47	ferry boat	det. *mẖnt* 'ferry-boat'
F48	boat with sail furled	det. boat, sail (downstream)
F49	boat under sail	det. sail (upstream)
F50	processional boat of Osiris	det. *nšmt* 'the Neshmet-boat of Osiris'
F51	processional boat of Osiris	alternative form of F50
F52	boat of Sokar	det. festivals for the god Soker
F53	sledge	2c. *tm*
F54	elephant tusk	(1) 2c. *bḥ*; (2) 2c. *ḥw*
F55	gaming board	2c. *mn*
F56	seal with necklace	ideo. *ḥtmty* 'seal-bearer', alternative for D38
F57	gold collar	(1) ideo. *nbw* 'gold'; (2) hence det. precious metal

Reference tables

Verb forms

The focus of this book is on reading actual monuments, rather than struggling through a morass of grammar. Nevertheless, a sizeable area of Egyptian grammar has also been covered. The reference tables provided here cover the grammar as presented in this book and are for quick reference and comparison.

Verb classes (§30)

Middle Egyptian verb-forms show differences in their writing according to the type of the verb. The following are the four basic verb classes:

STRONG VERBS	e.g.		*sḏm*	hear	stem does not usually show any alteration
DOUBLING VERBS	e.g.		*m33*	see	stem ends in a double consonant
WEAK VERBS	e.g.		*mr(i)*	love	stem ends with a 'weak' consonant, usually *-i*
EXTRA WEAK VERBS	e.g.		*rd(i)*	give	chiefly verbs with two or three weak consonants

Notes

  i With weak verbs, the final *-i* is usually omitted in writing and therefore in transliteration, though for practical reasons we normally transliterate 'give' as *rdi*.

 ii Extra weak verbs behave like ordinary weak verbs, but sometimes show additional features.

The infinitive (§31)

INFINITIVE

STRONG - no change		*sḏm*	hearing, to hear
DOUBLING - doubling		*m33*	seeing, to see
WEAK - end in *-t*		*mrt*	loving, to love
EXTRA WEAK - end in *-t*	or	*rdit/dit* (*r* optional)	giving, to give

The infinitive of strong verbs shows no specific writing, whereas weak verbs show a final -*t*.

Main tenses appearing in this book

The past tense (§§33 and 38)

$sḏm.n(=f)$

STRONG		$sḏm.n=f$	he heard
DOUBLING - no doubling		$mꜣ.n=f$	he saw
WEAK		$mr.n=f$	he loved
EXTRA WEAK		$(r)di.n=f$ (*r* optional)	he gave

The present tense: general present sḏm(=f) and specific present ḥr sḏm (§§42–43)

GENERAL PRESENT
$sḏm(=f)$

STRONG		$sḏm=f$	he hears
DOUBLING - doubling		$mꜣꜣ=f$	he sees
WEAK		$mr=f$	he loves
EXTRA WEAK		$di=f$ (no *r*)	he gives

SPECIFIC PRESENT
$ḥr sḏm$

STRONG		$ḥr sḏm$	is listening
DOUBLING		$ḥr mꜣꜣ$	is looking
WEAK		$ḥr mrt$	is loving
EXTRA WEAK		$ḥr rdit$	is giving

The specific present is made up of 𓁹𓂋 *ḥr* followed by the infinitive.

The future tense (wishes, requests, expectations): the future sḏm(=f) (§§55-57, §59)

FUTURE sḏm(=f)

STRONG		sḏm=f	may he hear
DOUBLING - no doubling		mꜣ=f	may he see
WEAK	or	mr=f or mry=f	may he love
EXTRA WEAK		dі=f (no r)	may he give
SPECIAL CASES		іwt=f (with extra -t)	may he come
		іnt=f (with extra -t)	may he bring

Notes

 i   The verb *mꜣꜣ* 'to see' also displays a form ⟨glyphs⟩ *mꜣn=f.*

 ii The weak verb form with ⟨glyphs⟩ *-y* is most common in the first person.

 iii Notice that the forms from the verbs 'to come' and 'to bring' show an extra *t* in the future *sḏm(=f)* form.

Negation (§§ 39 and 58)

The three principal tenses above are negated as follows:

NEGATIONS

PRESENT TENSE		n sḏm.n=f	he does not hear, he cannot hear
PAST TENSE		n sḏm=f	he did not hear
FUTURE TENSE		nn sḏm=f	may he not hear, he will not hear

The future is negated by adding the negation ⟨glyphs⟩ *nn* to the future *sḏm(=f)* form. However, the present and past tense negatives display a most unusual apparent reversal – known as *Gunn's rule* – where ***n sḏm.n(=f)*** negates the present *sḏm(=f)*, not the past *sḏm.n(=f)*, and ***n sḏm(=f)*** negates the past *sḏm.n(=f)*, not the *sḏm(=f)*. In fact, the *sḏm(=f)* in this construction shows a special form:

$n \ s\underline{d}m=f$

STRONG VERBS		$n \ s\underline{d}m=f$	he did not hear
DOUBLING VERBS - no doubling		$n \ m^{33}=f$	he did not see
WEAK VERBS		$n \ mr=f$	he did not love
EXTRA WEAK VERBS		$n \ rdi=f$ (with *r*)	he did not give

So, the present and past tense negatives are better thought of as constructions in their own right with their own grammar, rather than just as *sḏm(=f)* and *sḏm.n(=f)* with ‿ *n* stuck in front of them.

Specialised forms: the participles, relative forms and *sḏmty.fy*

The participles (§§46–51)

	PRESENT OR INCOMPLETE			PAST OR COMPLETE		
STRONG		*sḏm*	(one) who hears		*sḏm*	(one) who heard
DOUBLING		*m³³*	(one) who sees		*m³*	(one) who saw
WEAK		*mrr*	(one) who loves		*mr*	(one) who loved
EXTRA WEAK		*dd* (no *r*)	(one) who gives		*rdi* (with *r*)	(one) who gave

Participles also sometimes show a ⟨⟩ -*w* ending.

The relative forms (§§37 and 52)

	PRESENT OR INCOMPLETE			PAST OR COMPLETE		
STRONG		*sḏmt=f*	what he hears		*sḏmt.n=f*	what he heard
DOUBLING		*m³³t=f*	what he sees		*m³t.n=f*	what he saw
WEAK		*mrrt=f*	what he loves		*mrt.n=f*	what he loved
EXTRA WEAK		*ddt=f*	what he gives		*rdit.n=f*	what he gave

Compare with the corresponding forms of the participles.

The relative forms here display the *-t* of feminine adjectival agreement. They can also occur in certain usages without the *-t* (i.e. with masculine adjectival agreement), though they still carry the same meaning of 'which someone does/did'. See §52.

The *sḏmty.fy* form (§§53-54, §59)

sḏmty.fy

STRONG VERBS		*sḏmty.fy*	(one) who may/will hear
DOUBLING VERBS		*mꜣꜣty.fy*	(one) who may/will see
WEAK VERBS		*šdty.fy*	(one) who may/will read
EXTRA WEAK VERBS		*rdity.fy*	(one) who may/will give

Pronouns, nouns and adjectives

Suffix pronouns (§§33, 35, 36)

I	or	*=i*		we		*=n*
you		*=k*		you (pl.)	or	*=ṯn or =tn*
you (fem.)	or	*=ṯ or =t*				
he/it		*=f*		they	or	*=sn*
she/it	or	*=s*				

Uses:
a. as the subject after a suffix-conjugation verb-form, such as *sḏm.n(=f)*
b. as the object after a preposition.
c. after auxiliaries.
d. as the possessor or genitive of nouns.

The suffix pronouns translate as the appropriate English pronoun, so or =*i* translates as 'I' or 'me' or 'my' depending on English usage (and so on for the other pronouns). The use of 'I', 'you' etc. in the tables above and below is merely to point out the person or thing the pronoun refers to.

Dependent pronouns (§41)

I	[glyphs] or [glyph]	*-wi* or *-w(i)*	we	[glyphs]	*-n*	
you	[glyphs] or [glyphs]	*-tw* or *-tw*	you (pl.)	[glyphs] or [glyph]	*-tn* or *-tn*	
you (fem.)	[glyph] or [glyph]	*-tn* or *-tn*				
he/it	[glyphs] or [glyphs]	*-sw*	they	[glyphs] or [glyph]	*-sn*	
she/it	[glyphs] or [glyph]	*-sy* or *-s(y)*	it, they	[glyph]	*-st*	

-st is used for indefinite 'it' and generally as the dependent pronoun form for 'they/them'.

Uses:

a. Object of the verb (except the infinitive, which usually takes a suffix pronoun object).

b. After initial particles and the negation [glyph] *nn*.

Independent pronouns (§49)

I	[glyph] or [glyphs]	*ink*	We	[glyphs]	*inn*
you	[glyph]	*ntk*	you (pl)	[glyphs] or [glyphs]	*nttn* or *nttn*
you (fem.)	[glyph] or [glyph]	*ntt* or *ntt*			
he/it	[glyph]	*ntf*	they	[glyphs] or [glyphs]	*ntsn*
she/it	[glyph] or [glyph]	*nts*			

Uses: As the subject of characterisations.

Nouns (§§8, 9, 15)

Nouns have a number (singular or plural) and a gender (masculine or feminine); the *-w* of the plural is often omitted in writing:

SG. MSC.	no special ending		[glyph]	*sn*	brother
SG. FEM.	[glyph]	*-t*	[glyph]	*snt*	sister
PL. MSC.	[glyph]	*-w*	[glyph]	*snw*	brothers
PL. FEM.	[glyph]	*-wt*	[glyph]	*snwt*	sisters

The dual ending msc. *-wy* and fem. *-ty* is common only with things which come in pairs:

[glyph] *ꜥwy* arms   [glyph] *tꜣwy* the two lands (Upper and Lower Egypt)

Adjectives (§§10, 44-45)

Adjectives follow the noun they describe and agree with it in number and gender:

SG. MSC.		no special ending
SG. FEM.	⌒	-t
PL. MSC.	𓅂	-w
PL. FEM.	⌒	-t

The plural can also be written with the plural strokes, and the -w is often omitted in writing.

Adjectives can be used on their own as a noun, e.g.:

𓄤𓏏 *nfrt* the good (n.) from 𓄤 *nfr* good (adj.)

The genitive (§27)

Direct genitive: common only between closely connected words or in fixed expressions.

Indirect genitive: the two nouns are linked by forms of the 'genitival adjective' *n*:

	SINGULAR		PLURAL	
MASCULINE	〰	*n*	ⵔ or 〰	*nw* or *n*
FEMININE	〰⌒	*nt*	〰⌒	*nt*

Adjectives in -y (§60)

SG. MSC.	\\	-y	𓇋𓅓𓅯	*imy*	who/which is in
SG. FEM.	⌒	-t	𓇋𓅓	*imt*	who/which is in
PL. MSC.	𓅂	-w	𓇋𓅓𓅯𓅂	*imw*	who/which are in
PL. FEM.	⌒	-t	𓇋𓅓	*imt*	who/which are in

Egyptian–English vocabulary

Here, as in other Egyptian dictionaries, words are listed alphabetically in transliteration following the order set out in List 1 (the only exception being that the feminine ending -*t* is ignored, e.g. *s* 'man' and *st* 'woman' are listed together). In other words, the particular hieroglyphs used to write a word do not determine where it is listed. So to find a word, you need to know its reading in transliteration: if necessary, consult the various sign-lists. For example, imagine you come across the word 𓎛𓏏 but do not recognise its constituent signs. There are two stages in tracking down its meaning: (1) If you turn to List V beginning on p. 129, you will find 𓎛 (B62) has the reading *ḥsf*, whilst 𓊡 (F49) is not a sound-sign but a determinative for 'sail upstream'; so the reading of the whole word is *ḥsf*. (2) Returning to this vocabulary, you will find in the section headed *ḥ* that there are two words read *ḥsf* : 'repel' and 'travel upstream' (see p. 158). Of course, the determinative indicates that the second of these is the correct meaning, although, more often than not, the context in which the word occurs will also help you decide which of the two is correct. Although the hieroglyphic writings given in this list are representative of what you may find, it is not possible to list all of the ways in which a word could be written (see §14 again, if you are not yet sure about this). The following abbreviations have been used here: (a.) adjective; (n.) noun; (v.) strong verb; (w.v.) weak verb; (f.) feminine; (pl.) plural.

ꜣ

ꜣw (a.) long; joyful

ꜣbt (n.) family, household

ꜣbd (n.) month; monthly festival

ꜣbḏw Abydos (place name)

ꜣpd (n.) bird

ꜣryt (n.) staff

ꜣḫ (v.) become an akh-spirit; be useful

(n.) akh-spirit

ꜣst (the goddess) Isis (see p. 70)

ꜣsir (the god) Osiris; possibly read *wsir*

i

=*i* I, me, my (suffix pronoun, p. 148)

i O! (interjection) (§54a)

iꜣt (n.) office, function

iꜣ(w) (n.) praise, adoration

iꜣw (a.) old; (n.) old age

iy(i) (w.v.) come

iiw welcome
see also *iw(i)*

iꜥḥ (n.) moon

iw see §34

iw(i) (w.v.) come

iw welcome
see also *iy(i)*

iw(i) (w.v.) be boatless

iww (n.) boatless person

iwꜣ (n.) ox

iwꜣ(w) (n.) cattle

iwit (n.) wrongdoing

iwn (n.) pillar.

iwnw Heliopolis (place-name)

iwri Iuri (name)

ib (n.) heart; see also *ḥrt-ib, st-ib*

ib(i) (w.v.) be thirsty

ib thirsty
person

ip (v.) count, inspect

imꜣ (a.) charming, gracious
(the writing indicates the reading
has become *iꜣm* or *im*)

imꜣḫ (n.) reverence

or   or   *imꜣḫy*
or *imꜣḫw* (n.) revered one.

or   *imy* (a.) who/which is
in (§60)

imy-wt 'the one who is
in the *wt*', i.e. Anubis (title)

imy-ḫnt chamberlain
(title)

imn (the god) Amun

imn-m-ḥꜣt
Amenemhet (name)

imn-rꜥ (the god)
Amun-Re

imny Ameny (name)

imnt (n.) west

imnty (a.) western; for
imntw people of the west, see *ḫnt*

imsti (the god) Imseti, one of
the sons of Horus.

in by (§28); 'it is' (§51)

in(i) (w.v.) bring

inw (n.) produce, gifts

in-ḥrt-nḫt
Inhuretnakht (name)

inpw (the god) Anubis

ink I (independent pronoun, §49)

intf Intef (name)

ir(i) (w.v.) do, make; plus many
idomatic meanings

ir-n made by, i.e. born of

iry (a.) relating to (§60)

iry (n.) keeper

iry-nfr-ḥꜣt (title)
keeper of the king's diadem

is (n.) tomb

iḳr (a.) excellent, effective,
astute

iḳdw (n.) builders; see *ḳd*

or   *it* (n.) father

it(w) (n.) forefathers

it-nṯr god's father (title)

ity (n.) sovereign

ity Ity (name)

itn (n.) sun-disc; (the god)
Aten

꘎ or ꘎ *iṯ(i)* (w.v.) seize (the latter writing indicates the reading has become *iṯ*)

꘎ *ꜥ*

꘎ *ꜥ* (n.) arm; note ꘎ \\ *ꜥwy* arms; see also *ẖry-ꜥ, st-ꜥ, tp-ꜥ*

꘎ *ꜥꜣ* (a.) great

꘎ *ꜥꜣ(w)* (n.) the great (in society)

꘎ *ꜥꜣt* in *n-ꜥꜣt-n* because of

꘎ *ꜥmꜥꜣ* (v.) throw (a throw-stick)

꘎ *ꜥnḫ* (v.) live; (n.) life

꘎ *ꜥnḫ ḏt* living for all time

꘎ *ꜥnḫw* (n.) the living

꘎ *ꜥnḫt nṯr im* on which a god lives (§26)

꘎ *di ꜥnḫ* given life

꘎ *ꜥnḫ-n-nwt* (n.) local soldier

꘎ *ꜥḥ* (n.) palace

꘎ *ꜥḥꜣ* (v.) fight; (n.) fighting

꘎ *ꜥḥꜥ* (v.) stand

꘎ *ꜥẖnwty* variant form of *ꜥẖnwty*

꘎ *ꜥẖnwty* (n.) chamber; *m-r ꜥẖnwty* overseer of the chamber (title)

꘎ *ꜥḳyt* (n.) entering maid

꘎ *w*

꘎ or ꘎ *wꜣt* (n.) road, way

꘎ or ꘎ *wꜣst* Thebes (place-name)

꘎ *wꜣg* (n.) the Wag-festival

꘎ or ꘎ *-wi* I, me (dependent pronoun, p. 149)

꘎ *wꜥ* (a.) one, alone

꘎ *wꜥꜥw* (n.) privacy

꘎ *wꜥb* (a.) pure

꘎ *wꜥb* (n.) pure one, i.e. *wꜥb*-priest

꘎ or ꘎ *wbꜣ* (n.) cup-bearer

꘎ *wbꜣt* (fem.) cup-bearer

꘎ *wp(i)* (w.v.) open, separate

꘎ *wp-wꜣwt* (the god) Wepwawet

꘎ *wn* (v.) open

꘎ *wnwt* (n.) priesthood

꘎ *wnn* (v.) be, exist; *n-wn-mꜣꜥ* truly, truthfully.

꘎ *wnn-nfr* (the god) Wenennefer, i.e. Osiris

꘎ *wr* (a.) great, important

꘎ *wr(w)* (n.) the great (in society)

꘎ *wrt* (n.) the great bark

꘎ *wḥm* (v.) repeat; reporter, herald (title)

꘎ *wsr* (a.) powerful

꘎ *wsrt* Wosret (name), literally 'powerful one' and may be used as a designation for female deities

꘎ *wt* see *imy*

꘎ *wḏ* (v.) order; (n.) order

꘎ *wḏꜣ* (v.) set out, proceed

꘎ *b*

꘎ or ꘎ *bꜣ* (n.) ba-spirit

bꜣ-mkt Bameket (name)

bꜣḥ see *m-bꜣḥ*

bꜣk (n.) servant (see p. 101)

bin (a.) bad

or *bity* (n.) king

bnr (a.) pleasant

bt Bet (name)

□ *p*

pt (n.) sky

pꜣt (n.) antiquity, beginning of time

pw it is, this is

pf that; (fem.) *tf*, (pl.) *nf*.

pn this; (fem.) *tn*, (pl.) *nn*.

pr (n.) estate

pr-ꜥꜣ (n.) palace

m-r pr overseer of an estate, steward
see also *nbt-pr*, *r-pr*

pr(i) (w.v.) go out

prt (n.) procession

prt-ḥrw (n.) voice-offering

or *pḥty* (a.) strength

pkr Poker (place-name); see also *r-pkr*

ptḥ (the god) Ptah

ptḥ-ḥtp Ptahhotep (name)

or *ptr* (v.) observe, view

f

=f he, him, his (suffix pronoun, p. 148)

m

m in

m-bꜣḥ in the presence of

or *m-m* among

or *m-r* (n.) overseer; for specific titles, e.g. *m-r pr*, see the second element

mꜣꜣ (v.) see, look at

mꜣi-n-ḥr Maienhor (name)

mꜣꜥ (v.) present, guide

or *mꜣꜥ* (v.) be true, right, proper; (a.) true; for *n-wn-mꜣꜥ* see *wn*

mꜣꜥ-ḥrw (a.) true of voice, justified; (v.) be justified

or *mꜣꜥt* (n.) what is proper, i.e. truth, harmony; (the goddess) Maat, often written

mi as, like

or *mity* (n.) equal, peer

mꜥḥꜥt (n.) cenotaph, tomb

mꜥk (v.) roast

mw (n.) water

mwt (n.) mother

mnꜥt (n.) wet-nurse

mnw dedication, monument (see p. 126)

mnw (the god) Min

mnw-nfr Minnefer (name)

⬚⬚⬚ or ⬚⬚ *mnḫt* (n.) linen

⬚⬚ *mnṯw* (the god) Montju

⬚⬚⬚ *mnṯw-ḥtp* Mentjuhotep (name)

⬚⬚ *mr(i)* (w.v.) want, love

⬚⬚ or ⬚ *mrḥt* (n.) oil, unguent

⬚⬚ *mrs* Meres (name)

⬚⬚ *mrti* Merti (name)

⬚⬚ *mḫnt* (n.) ferry

⬚⬚ *ms* (v.) bring, present

⬚⬚ *m-sȝ=f* Emsaf (name)

⬚⬚ *ms(i)* (w.v.) give birth

⬚⬚ *ms-n* born of

⬚⬚ *msw* (n.) offspring

⬚⬚ *msḏ(i)* (w.v.) hate

⬚⬚ *mšʿ* (n.) expedition, army

⬚⬚ *mdḥw* Medhu (name)

⬚ *n*

⬚ *=n* we, us, our (suffix pronoun, p. 148), *-n* we, us (dependent pronoun, p. 149)

⬚ *n* to, for; for negative *n* (§39); for *n-ʿȝt-n* see ʿȝ ; for *n-wn-mȝʿ* see *wn*

⬚ *n* of (§27); ⬚ (f.) *nt*; ○ (pl.) *nw*

⬚ negative *n* (§39)

⬚ *n sp* never

⬚ *nis* (v.) call out, summon

○ *nw* see *n*

⬚ *nwt* (the goddess) Nut

⬚ *nwt* (n.) town, city; see also *nṯr*

⬚ *nb* all, every (§16)

⬚ *nb* (n.) lord (§16)

⬚ *nbt* (n.) lady

⬚ *nbt pr* (n.) lady of the house, mistress of the estate, i.e. woman of high status

⬚ *nb(=i)-pw-snwsrt* Nebipusenusret (name)

⬚ or ⬚ *nbt-ḥwt* (the goddess) Nephthys

⬚ *nbw* (n.) gold

⬚ *n-ptḥ-kȝw* Niptahkau (name)

⬚ *nf* see *pf*

⬚ *nfr* (a.) perfect, good, wonderful, beautiful

⬚ *nfrw* (n.) perfection, splendour

⬚ or ⬚ *nmtt* (n.) step, formal journey

⬚ *nn* see *pn*

⬚ *nn* without; future negation (§58)

⬚ *nnwy* Nenwy (name)

⬚ or ⬚ *nḥḥ* (n.) (for) eternity

⬚ *nḫnt* (n.) youth

⬚ *nḫt* (a.) strong, vigorous

⬚ *nḫti* Nakhti (name)

⬚ *nḫt-ʿnḫ* Nakhtankh (name)

⬚ *nsw* (n.) king (§23)

⬚ *nsw-bity* king of the dualities, king of Upper and Lower Egypt (royal title)

⬚ *nšt* (n.) hairdresser

⬚ *nšmt* (n.) Neshmet-bark, the processional boat of Osiris

⬚ *ngȝw* (n.) long-horned bull

nt-nbw Netnebu (name)

nṯr (n) god

nṯrw nwtw town-gods

nṯr nfr the perfect god (royal title) (§17)

ndyt Nedyet (place-name)

nḏ (v.) protect

nḏm (a.) sweet

nḏs (a.) small

nḏs (n.) person, individual

nḏs(w) (n.) the lowly

r

r towards, at; more than (p, 81); in order to (p. 84); for words compounded with *r* see under the second element, e.g. *r-ḥꜣt*, etc.

r (n.) mouth

r-pr (n.) temple complex

r-pḳr Ro-Poker (place-name); see also *pḳr*

or   *rꜥ* (n.) day; sun; (the god) Ra or Re

or   *rm(w)* (n.) fish

rmṯ (n.) people

rn (n.) name

rnpt (n.) year

rnpt-sp (n.) regnal year

tp-rnpt (n.) festival of the beginning of the lunar year

rrwt Rerut (name)

rḫ (v.) know, learn

or   *rḫ-nsw* king's adviser, king's confidant (title)

rḫty (n.) washerman

rd or *rwd* (n.) terrace

or   *rd(i)* (w.v.) give, put; cause (§40)

rdwy (n.) legs, feet

h

hꜣ(i) (w.v.) descend

hꜣb (v.) send

hꜣkr (n.) Haker-rites (at Abydos)

hi (n.) husband

hbny (n.) ebony

hnw (n.) jubilation

hrw (n.) day, daytime

ḫrt-hrw daily course

ḥ

ḥꜣt (n.) front

r-ḥꜣt before

ḥr-ḥꜣt before

ḥꜣy (a.) naked

(n.) naked person

ḥꜣty-ꜥ (n.) governor, mayor

ḥꜥpy (n.) Nile inundation (often personified as the god Hapy)

ḥwt (n.) enclosure, foundation

ḥwt-nṯr (n.) temple

ḥwt-ḥr (the goddess) Hathor

ḥw(i) (w.v.) beat

ḥwt (n.) beating

ḥwi Hui (name)

or ḥb (n.) festival

ḥbs (v.) clothe

ḥbsw (n.) clothing

ḥpt (n.) oar

ḥpy (the god) Hapy, i.e. one of the sons of Horus

ḥm (n.) person (§18)

ḥm-nṯr (n.) ḥm-priest

ḥmt-nṯr (f.) ḥm-priestess

ḥm-kꜣ (n.) ka-priest

ḥmt (n.) wife

ḥnꜥ together with

or ḥnḳt (n.) beer (§23)

ḥr (the god) Horus; as king's name (§17)

ḥr (n.) face

ḥr on, at; because of; usually written before suffixes; as verbal auxiliary (§42)

ḥry (a) who/which is upon (§60)

ḥry-pr (n.) domestic servant

ḥrt-pr (fem.) domestic servant

or ḥry-sštꜣ (n.) master of secrets

ḥry-tp (n.) chief, superior

see nḥḥ

ḥs(i) (w.v.) praise

ḥst (n.) favour

ḥsb (n.) counter

ḥsmn (n.) amethyst

ḥḳt (the goddess) Heket

ḥkꜣ (v.) rule

ḥkꜣ (n.) ruler

ḥḳr (v.) hunger

(n.) hungry person

ḥtp (v.) content, satisfy, rest, be content; (n.) peace, satisfaction; (n.) offering; (n.) altar; Hetep (name)

ḥtp-nṯr (n.) divine offerings

ḥtpt offerings

ḥtp di nsw (n.) an offering which the king gives (§26)

ḫ

ḫt (n.) thing, things

ḫꜣ (n.) thousand

ḫw Khu (name)

ḫwyt Khuyt (name)

ḫw-n-bik Khuenbik (name)

ḫpt (n.) death

ḫpr (v.) become; (n.) form, being

ḫpš (n.) foreleg, strong arm

ḫfty (n.) enemy

ḫnm (v.) gladden

ḫnms (n.) friend

ḫnt in front

ḫnty (a.) who/which is in front, foremost (§60)

ḫnty-imntw Khentyimentu, i.e. 'foremost of the westerners' (name of Osiris) ẖnty sḥ-nṯr 'the one in front at the god's booth' (epithet of Anubis)

see *imy-ẖnt*

ẖntyt Khentyt (place-name)

ẖnt-ẖnty-ḥtp Khenetkhentyhetep (name)

ẖr before, in front of

ẖr (v.) fall

ẖrt-ib (n.) wish, preference; see *st*

ẖrw (n.) voice; for *mꜣꜥ-ẖrw* see *mꜣꜥ*

ẖrp (v.) control; director (title)

ẖsf (v.) repel, ward off

ẖsf(w) (w.v.) travel upstream, travel south; see also *ẖd(i)*

ẖtm (n.) seal

ẖtmw ẖry-ꜥ seal-bearer, assistant (title)

ẖtmty-bity seal-bearer of the king (title)

m-r ẖtmt treasurer (title)

ẖd(i) (w.v.) travel north, travel downstream; see also *ẖsf(w)*

ẖ

ẖnw (n.) interior; the interior, i.e. the palace

r-ẖnw inside

ẖnm (v.) join; (a.) united with (m)

ẖnmw (the god) Khnum

ẖr under, carrying

ẖry (a.) who/which is under (§60)

ẖry-ꜥ (n.) deputy, assistant;

ẖry-ḥbt (n.) lector-priest

ẖry-tp chamberlain (title)

ẖrt (n.) share, duty

ẖrt-hrw (n.) daily course

or   ẖrt-nṯr (n.) cemetery

ẖrd (n.) child

ẖkrt-nsw lady-in-waiting (title)

or   —   s

or   —   =s she, her (suffix pronoun, p. 148)

s (n.) man

st (n.) woman

-st she, her, it, they (dependent pronoun, p. 149)

st (n.) place, position, status

st-ib (n.) affection, intimacy

st-ꜥ (n.) ability

st-ẖrt-ib (n.) confidence

m-r st overseer of the storehouse (title)

see *smyt* (§23)

sꜣ (n.) son

sꜣt (n.) daughter

sꜣ-imn Saamun (name)

sꜣt-wsrt Satwosret (name)

sꜣ-mnẖt Samenkhet (name)

sꜣt-mnṯw Satmontju (name)

sꜣ-rnnwtt Sarenenutet (name)

sꜣ-ḥwt-ḥr Sahathor (name)

sꜣ-ḫnt-ḫty Sakhentkhety (name)

sꜣt-ḫnt-ḫti Satkhentkheti (name)

sꜣt-sbk Satsobek (name)

sꜣwtyt Sautyt (name)

sꜣḫ (v.) transform into an akh-spirit, transfigure

-sy she, her, it (dependent pronoun, p. 149)

sꜥꜣ (v.) promote, advance

sꜥnḫ (v.) perpetuate (name)

or -sw he, him (dependent pronoun, p. 149)

or swꜣ (v.) pass by, surpass

swꜥb (v.) decorate

swḏ (v.) bequeath

or sbi (v.) rebel; sbi (n.) rebel

sbk (the god) Sobek

sp (n.) moment, deed; for n sp see n; for rnpt-sp see rnpt

spꜣt (n.) district.

sp(i) (w.v.) bind (together)

spḥ (v.) lassoo

spdt (the goddess) Sothis

sfṯw or sftw (n.) butcher

smi (w.v.) report; (n.) report

smyt (n.) desert (see §23)

smr (n.) courtier, royal companion

smr wꜥt(y) (n.) sole companion

smḥ (n.) papyrus skiff

smsw (a.) elder, eldest

or =sn they, them, their (suffix pronoun, p. 148); -sn they, them (dependent pronoun, p. 149)

sn (n.) brother

snt (n.) sister

snw snwt (n.) siblings, brothers and sisters

sn (v.) kiss

s-n-wsrt Senwosret (name)

snb (n.) health; (a.) healthy

snbi Senbi (name)

snfr (v.) improve

snt Senet (name)

snṯr (n.) incense

sr (n.) official

srw (n.) goose

srḫ (v.) complain about, accuse

sḫ in ḫnty sḫ-nṯr, see under ḫnt

sḥtp (v.) satisfy; see also ḥtp

sḥtp-ib Sehetepib (name)

sḫt (n.) countryside

sḫm (v.) control

sḫnt (v.) promote, augment

sḫr (v.) fell, overturn

sḫr (n.) conduct, plan

sḫsf (v.) (keep at a) distance

sš (n.) scribe; possibly to be read sš

sšm (n.) procedure, conduct

sštȝ (a.) secret; see also *ḥry-sštȝ*

skbḥ (v.) relax, calm down

skd(i) (w.v.) travel, sail

skr (the god) Soker

st (n.) scent; originally *sty*

st(i) (w.v.) shoot, spear

stp (v.) choose; (a.) chosen

sḏȝ (v.) travel, depart

sḏm (v.) hear, listen; the alternative ⌐ indicates that the reading had become *sḏm*

sḏrt (n.) vigil

š

šw (v.) be free from (*m*)

šw (the god) Shu

špsy (a.) dignified, wealthy

šps-nsw (n.) dignitary of the king

špswt (n.) dignity

špss (n.) wealth, dignity

šmꜥ (n.) Upper Egypt

šms (v.) follow

šmsw (n.) follower, attendant

šmsw (n.) following

šn (divine epithet) in Hor-*šn*, a name of Horus

šnyt (n.) entourage

šnwt (n.) granary

šnꜥw (n.) magazine, provisioning area

or   *šs* (n.) alabaster (calcite)

šsp (v.) receive

ḳ

ḳis Qis (Cusae) (place-name)

ḳbw Kebu (name)

ḳbḥ-snw=f (the god) Qebehsenuf, i.e. one of the sons of Horus

or   *ḳmȝ* (v.) create

ḳrs (v.) bury

ḳrst burial

ḳd (v.) build; see also *iḳdw*

k

=k you, your (suffix pronoun, p. 148)

kȝ (n.) ka-spirit

or   *kȝ* (n.) ox, bull

ky Key (name)

g

gb (the god) Geb

gm(i) (w.v.) find

grḥ (n.) night

t

=t you, your (f.) (see *=ṯ*)

or   *t* (n.) bread

tȝ (n.) land

tȝwy (n.) the two lands, i.e. Upper and Lower Egypt

tȝ-wr the nome of Thinis (place-name)

-tw you (see *-ṯw*)

tp (n.) head

　tp-ʿ (n.) ancestor
(for *ḥry-tp* see *ḥry* ; for *ḥry-tp* see
ḥry; for *tp-rnpt* see *rnpt*)

or 　*tpy* (a.) who/which is upon,
chief (§60)

　tpy ḏw=f 'the one who is
upon his mountain' (title of
Anubis)

tf see *pf*

tfnt (the goddess) Tefenet

tn see *pn*

=tn, -tn you, your (pl.) (see *=ṯn,
-ṯn*)

ṯ

=ṯ you, your (f.) (suffix pronoun,
p. 148)

ṯȝw (n.) breath, wind

ṯȝw Tjau (name)

=ṯn you, your (pl.) (suffix
pronoun, p. 148);
-ṯn you (pl.) (dependent pronoun,
p. 149)

-ṯw you (dependent pronoun,
p. 149)

ṯs(i) (w.v.) tie, knot, assign

ṯsw (n.) sandbank

d

or *d(i)* (w.v.) give; see *rd(i)*

ddt Dedet (name)

dwȝ (v.) adore

or
dwȝ-mwt=f (the god) Duamutef,
one of the sons of Horus

dbi Debi (name)

dbḥt-ḥtp (n.) required
offerings

dpt (n.) boat

ḏ

ḏt (n.) (for) all time, enduringly;
see also under *ʿnḫ*

ḏȝt (n.) wrongdoing

ḏȝ(i) (w.v.) cross, ferry

ḏȝt (n.) boat-journey

ḏw (n.) mountain; for *tpy ḏw=f* see
tpy

ḏws (v.) denounce

ḏʿm (n.) electrum

or *ḏf(ȝw)* (n.) provisions

ḏfȝ-ḥʿpy Djefahapy
(name)

ḏḥwty (the god) Thoth

ḏḥwtt (n.) the festival
of Thoth

ḏr since

ḏr-ntt because

ḏs self; used in conjunction with
suffix pronoun, *ḏs=i* 'myself', etc

ḏsr (v.) separate, clear; (a.) sacred

tȝ ḏsr the sacred land
(place-name)

ḏd (v.) say, speak

or *ḏdw* Djedu (place-
name)

Reading uncertain

?-nt (n.) half-month festival,
perhaps read *mḏdint* or *smdt* (see
p. 76)

Key to the exercises

Chapter 1

1.1 Kings' names:

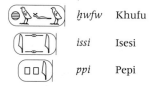

ḫwfw   Khufu

issi   Isesi

ppi   Pepi

1.2 Words from the roasting scene:

mꜥk   *srw*

1.3 Gods' names:

inpw   *ḥḳt*

ptḥ   *sbk*

rꜥ   *skr*

1.4 Transliterating words:

nḏs   *rn*

ḥb   *bin*

ꜣpd   *iḳr*

ꜥmꜥꜣ   *pḳr*

ꜣryt   *ḥd*

pt   *rm*

ḥbs   *šs*

ḫpš   *stt*

1.5 Writing out words in hieroglyphs:

ḫr   *ḥtm*

sr   *ḳrst*

1.6 Translation:

a.   *nḏs iḳr*   the/an astute individual   b.   *sḫr iḳr*   the/an excellent plan
c.   *ḥnꜥ snbi*   with Senbi   d.   *r pḳr*   to Poker

1.7 Translating the offering scene:

ḫpš n kꜣ n snbi mꜣꜥ-ḫrw   A foreleg for the ka of Senbi, the justified.

1.8 Study exercise: A fishing and fowling scene:

Above scene on left:
stt rm(w) in snbi mꜣꜥ-ḫrw
Spearing the fish by Senbi, the justified.

Above scene on right
ꜥmꜣꜣ r ꜣpd(w) in snbi mꜣꜥ-ḫrw
Throwing at the birds by Senbi, the justified.

Chapter 2

2.2 Words:

or	sȝ	or	kȝ
	wȝt		mr
	smr		wp
	ȝbḏw		ḏdw
	imn		ẖnmw
			wp-wȝwt

2.4 Expressions:

a.   nṯr ꜥȝ   great god

b.   ḫt nbt   everything
      nfrt wꜥbt   good and pure

2.6 Dating:

a.   *rnpt-sp 25 ḥr ḥm (n) nṯr nfr nb tȝwy*   Regnal year 25 under the person of the perfect
                                              god, the lord of the two lands

      n-mȝꜥt-rꜥ di ꜥnḫ mi rꜥ ḏt   Nimaatre, given life like Re enduringly.

b.   *rnpt-sp 14 ḥr ḥm n nsw-bity*   Regnal year 14 under the person of the king of
                                      Upper and Lower Egypt

      ḫpr-kȝ-rꜥ ꜥnḫ ḏt   Kheperkare, living enduringly.

c.   *rnpt-sp 13 ḥr ḥm n nsw-bity*   Regnal year 13 under the person of the king of
                                      Upper and Lower Egypt

      nbw-kȝw-rꜥ di ꜥnḫ ḏt r nḥḥ   Nubkaure, given life enduringly and
                                      repeatedly.

2.7 Study exercise: Middle Kingdom kings of the 12th dynasty:
The order of the first cartouche names should be as follows:

sḥtp-ib-rꜥ	(Amenemhet I)	*ḫꜥ-kȝw-rꜥ*	(Senwosret III)
ḫpr-kȝ-rꜥ	(Senwosret I)	*n-mȝꜥt-rꜥ*	(Amenemhet III)
nbw-kȝw-rꜥ	(Amenemhet II)	*mȝꜥ-ḫrw-rꜥ*	(Amenemhet IV)
ḫꜥ-ḫpr-rꜥ	(Senwosret II)	*sbk-kȝ-rꜥ*	(Nefrusobek)

2.8 Study exercise: New Kingdom pharaohs:
The New Kingdom pharaohs listed are:

nb-pḥty-rꜥ	*iꜥḥ-ms*	Ahmose
ḏsr-kȝ-rꜥ	*imn-ḥtp*	Amenhotep I
ꜥȝ-ḫpr-kȝ-rꜥ	*ḏḥwty-ms*	Thutmose I
ꜥȝ-ḫpr-n-rꜥ	*ḏḥwty-ms*	Thutmose II
mȝꜥt-kȝ-rꜥ	*ḥȝt-špswt ẖnmt-imn*	Hatshepsut
mn-ḫpr-rꜥ	*ḏḥwty-ms*	Thutmose III
ꜥȝ-ḫprw-rꜥ	*imn-ḥtp ḥkȝ-iwnw*	Amenhotep II
mn-ḫprw-rꜥ	*ḏḥwty-ms*	Thutmose IV
nb-mȝꜥt-rꜥ	*imn-ḥtp ḥkȝ-wȝst*	Amenhotep III
nfr-ḫprw-rꜥ wꜥ-n-rꜥ	*ȝḫ-n-itn*	Akhenaten
nb-ḫprw-rꜥ	*twt-ꜥnḫ-imn ḥkȝ-iwnw-šmꜥ*	Tutankhamun

ḏsr-ḫprw-rꜥ stp-n-rꜥ	*ḥr-m-ḥb mry-imn*	Horemheb
mn-pḥty-rꜥ	*rꜥ-ms-sw*	Ramesses I
mn-mꜣꜥt-rꜥ	*sty mry-n-ptḥ*	Seti I
wsr-mꜣꜥt-rꜥ stp-n-rꜥ	*rꜥ-ms-sw mry-imn*	Ramesses II
wsr-mꜣꜥt-rꜥ mry-imn	*rꜥ-ms-s(w) ḥkꜣ-iwnw*	Ramesses III

2.9 Study exercise: BM EA 117

The missing pharaohs are all the pharaohs of the 13th–17th dynasties inclusive, and within the 18th dynasty, Hatshepsut, Akhenaten and Tutankhamun (as well as the other Amarna pharaohs, Ay and the shadowy figure of Neferneferuaten/Smenkhkare).

Chapter 3

3.2 Words:

wr   *imny*

3.3 Gods' names:

ḫnty-imntw   *wnn-nfr*

3.4 Titles

m-r ꜥḥnwty   *smr-wꜥty*

3.6 The offering formula from BM EA 162:

ḥtp-di-nsw -	An offering which the king gives/places
ḥr ꜣsir ḫnty-imntw	before Osiris-Khentyimentu,
[nṭr ꜥꜣ nb] ꜣbḏw	[great god, lord] of Abydos,
m s(w)t=f nbt nfrt wꜥbt	in all his good and pure places,
di=f prt-ḫrw	so that he may give a voice offering
m t m ḥnḳt	in bread and in beer
m kꜣ ꜣpd m ḫt nb(t) nfrt	in ox and fowl and everything good
n kꜣ n imꜣḫw ḫr nṭr ꜥꜣ	for the ka of the revered one before the great god,
m-r mšꜥ wr imny	the general-in-chief Ameny,
ir-n ḳbw mꜣꜥ-ḫrw	born of Kebu, the justified.

3.7 Offering table scene:

dbḥt-ḥtp	The required offerings:
hꜣ(w) kꜣ ꜣpd ḫt nbt nfrt wꜥbt	thousands of ox and fowl and everything good and pure
n kꜣ n imꜣḫy	for the ka of the revered one,
ḥꜣty-ꜥ snbi mꜣꜥ-ḫrw	the governor Senbi, the justified.

3.8 Study exercise: BM EA 587

ḥtp-di-nsw	An offering which the king gives
ꜣsir nb ḏdw nṭr ꜥꜣ nb ꜣbḏw	to Osiris, lord of Djedu, great god, lord of Abydos,
prt-ḫrw	a voice offering of
t ḥnḳt kꜣ ꜣpd šs mnḫt	bread and beer, ox and fowl, alabaster and linen,
ḫt nbt nfr(t) wꜥb(t)	and everything good and pure
ꜥnḫt nṭr im	on which a god lives
n kꜣ n imꜣḫ(w)	for the ka of the revered one,
m-r ꜥḥnw(ty) imn-m-ḥꜣt	the overseer of the chamber Amenemhet, the justified.
mꜣꜥ-ḫrw	

3.9 Study exercise: BM EA 585

ḥtp-di-nsw	An offering which the king gives
ꜣsir nb ḏdw nṯr ꜥꜣ nb ꜣbḏw	to Osiris, lord of Djedu, great god, lord of Abydos,
di=f prt-ḫrw	so that he may give a voice offering of
t ḥnḳt kꜣ ꜣpd šs mnḫt	bread and beer, ox and fowl, alabaster and linen,
ḫt nbt ꜥnḫt nṯr im	and everything on which a god lives
n kꜣ n imꜣḫy	for the ka of the revered one,
dd ḥtp(w)-nṯr n nṯrw	the offering-giver to the gods,
ḥsb-šnwty m-r pr	the counter of the double granaries and steward
sꜣ-rnnwtt mꜣꜥ-ḫrw	Sarenenutet, the justified,
ms-n bꜣ-mkt	born of Bameket.

Chapter 4

Labels to the map of Abydos on p. 55:

rwd n nṯr ꜥꜣ	the terrace of the great god.
ḥwt-nṯr nt ꜣsir ḫnty-imntw	the temple of Osiris-Khentyimentu.
pḳr	Poker
tꜣ ḏsr	sacred land

4.2 Words:

𓊪𓏤𓈙𓏏𓀭	snt	𓎛𓅓𓏏𓀭	ḥmt
𓇼𓀢	dwꜣ	𓊪𓈙𓀁	sn
𓊪𓈙𓀗	sn	𓃂𓈙𓏏	wḥm

4.3 Translation:

Meir II, pl. 4:   sph ngꜣw
Lassooing the long-horned bull

Meir I, pl. 11:   wpt kꜣ(w)
Separating the bulls

4.4 Translating the captions on BM EA 101:

Centre:

ptr nfrw nṯr nfr	Seeing the splendour of the perfect god
ḫꜥ-kꜣw-rꜥ mꜣꜥ-ḫrw	Khakaure, the justified,
mry wp-wꜣwt nb tꜣ-ḏsr	beloved of Wepwawet, lord of the sacred land
mry ꜣsir wnn-nfr nb ꜣbḏw	beloved of Osiris-Wenennefer, lord of Abydos.

Right:

dwꜣ wp-wꜣwt m prt=f nfrt	Adoring Wepwawet during his wonderful procession
ḏt r nḥḥ	for ever and ever.

Left:

dwꜣ ꜣsir m ḥb(w)=f nfrw	Adoring Osiris during his wonderful festivals
ḏt r nḥḥ	for ever and ever.

4.5 Translating the captions on BM EA 581

Top:

sn tꜣ n ḫnty-imntw	Kissing the ground to Khentyimentu
mꜣꜣ nfrw wp-wꜣwt	and seeing the splendour of Wepwawet
in m-r ꜥḥnwty intf	by the overseer of the chamber Intef.

Bottom:

prt-ḫrw n imꜣḫ(w)	A voice-offering for the revered one
m-r ꜥḥnwty intf ir-n snt	the overseer of the chamber Intef, born of Senet.

4.6 Study exercise: Fishing and fowling scene from the tomb of Senbi at Meir

Left-hand scene:

stt rm(w)   Spearing fish
  in imзḥy ḥr зsir nb smyt imntt   by the revered one before Osiris, lord of the
                                                                    western desert,
    ḥзty-ꜥ m-r ḥm-nṯr   the governor and overseer of the priests
      snbi mзꜥ-ḥrw   Senbi, the justified.

Right-hand scene:

ꜥmꜥз r зpd(w)   Throwing at birds
  in ḥзty-ꜥ ḥtmty-bity   by the governor, seal-bearer of the king,
    smr wꜥty snbi mзꜥ-ḥrw   and sole companion Senbi, the justified.

Above Senbi's wife:

ḥmt=f n st-ib=f   His wife of his affection
    mrs nbt imзḥ   Meres, possessor of reverence.

4.7 Study exercise: The coffin of Nakhtankh (BM EA 35285)

Eastern side – horizontal inscription:

ḥtp-di-nsw   An offering which the king gives
  зsir nb ḏḏw ḫnty-imntw   to Osiris, lord of Djedu, Khentyimentu,
    nṯr ꜥз nb зbḏw   great god, lord of Abydos,
di=f ḥt nb(t) nfrt wꜥbt   so that he may give everything good and pure:
  ḥз m t ḥnkt   a thousand of bread and beer,
  kз зpd šs mnḥt   ox and fowl, alabaster and linen,
    ꜥnḥt nṯr im   on which a god lives,
n kз n imзḥ(y)   for the ka of the revered one,
  nḥt-ꜥnḥ mзꜥ-ḥrw   Nakhtankh, the justified.

Vertical inscriptions from north to south:

imзḥ(y) ḥr imsti nḥt-ꜥnḥ   The revered one before Imseti, Nakhtankh.
imзḥ(y) ḥr šw nḥt-ꜥnḥ mзꜥ-ḥrw   The revered one before Shu, Nakhtankh, the justified.
imзḥ(y) ḥr gb nḥt-ꜥnḥ mзꜥ-ḥrw   The revered one before Geb, Nakhtankh, the justified.
imзḥ(y) ḥr dwз-mwt=f nḥt-ꜥnḥ   The revered one before Duamutef, Nakhtankh, the
  mзꜥ-ḥrw   justified.

Western side – horizontal inscription:

ḥtp-di-nsw   An offering which the king gives
  inp(w) ḫnty sḥ-nṯr   to Anubis, the one before the divine booth,
    tp(y)-ḏw=f im(y)-wt   the one on his mountain, the one in the *wt*,
      nb tз-ḏsr   lord of the sacred land:
ḳrst nfrt m is=f nfr n ḥrt-nṯr   a good burial in his wonderful tomb of the necropolis;
  imзḥy ḥr nṯr ꜥз   the revered one before the great god,
    nḥt-ꜥnḥ mзꜥ-ḥrw   Nakhtankh, the justified.

Vertical inscriptions from north to south:

imзḥ(y) ḥr ḥpy nḥt-ꜥnḥ mзꜥ-ḥrw   The revered one before Hapy, Nakhtankh, the justified.
imзḥ(y) ḥr tfnt nḥt-ꜥnḥ mзꜥ-ḥrw The revered one before Tefnut, Nakhtankh, the justified.
imзḥ(y) ḥr nwt nḥt-ꜥnḥ mзꜥ-ḥrw   The revered one before Nut, Nakhtankh, the justified.
imзḥ(y) ḥr ḳbḥ-snw=f nḥt-ꜥnḥ   The revered one before Qebehsenuef, Nakhtankh, the
  mзꜥ-ḥrw   justified.

Chapter 5

5.2 Words:

	ḥst		ẖnms
	ḏꜣt		wḏꜣ
	ḥkꜣ		ḥsmn
	nmtt		iwit
	ḏꜣ(i)		

5.3 Translation:

a. *iw ir.n=i prt ꜥꜣt* — I conducted the great procession.
b. *iw ḳrs.n=i iꜣ(w)* — I buried the old.
c. *iw rdi.n(=i) t n ḥḳr ḥbsw n ḥꜣy* — I gave bread to the hungry and clothes to the naked.
d. *iw ḏꜣ.n(=i) iww m mẖnt(=i) ḏs(=i)* — I ferried the boatless in my own ferry.
e. *iw wḥm.n(=i) ḥst ḥr nsw* — I repeated favour before the king.

5.4 Study exercise: BM EA 1783

Lines 1-2:

ḥtp-di-nsw — An offering which the king gives
inpw tp(y)-ḏw=f — to Anubis, the one on his mountain,
im(y)-wt nb tꜣ-ḏsr — the one in the *wt*, lord of the sacred land:
prt-ḥrw n ḥꜣty-ꜥ — a voice offering for the governor,
ẖtmty-biti smr-wꜥt(y) — seal-bearer of the king, sole companion,
ẖry-ḥbt — and lector-priest,
imꜣẖw ẖr nṯr ꜥꜣ nb pt — and revered one before the great god and lord of the sky,
in-ḥrt-nẖt — Inhuretnakht.

Lines 4-5:

iw rdi.n(=i) t n ḥḳr — I gave bread to the hungry
ḥbsw n ḥꜣy — and clothes to the naked.
iw ḏꜣ.n(=i) iww <m> mẖnt(=i) ḏs(=i) — I ferried the boatless in my own ferry.
iw ir.n(=i) kꜣ(w) 100 m irt.n(=i) ḏs(=i) — I acquired 100 bulls through what I did myself.

The family:

ḥmt=f mrt=f ẖkrt-nsw-wꜥtt — His beloved wife, the sole lady-in-waiting
ḥm(t)-nṯr ḥwt-ḥr — and priestess of Hathor,
imꜣẖt ḥwi — the revered one Hui.
sꜣ=f mry=f nnwy — His beloved son Nenwy.

The dedication:

irt.n n=f sꜣ=f smsw=f mry=f dbi — What his beloved eldest son Debi made for him.

5.5 Study exercise: BM EA 571 (top)

First offering formula:

ḥtp-di-nsw — An offering which the king gives
ꜣsir nb ḏdw ẖnty-imntw — to Osiris, lord of Djedu, Khentyimentu,
nṯr ꜥꜣ nb ꜣbḏw — great god, lord of Abydos,
di=f prt-ḥrw t ḥnkt — so that he may give a voice offering of bread and beer,

ḫ3 m k3 3pd š3 mnḫt	a thousand of ox and fowl, alabaster and linen,
ḫt nb(t) nfr(t) wˁb(t)	and everything good and pure
ˁnḫt nṭr ˁ3 im	on which the great god lives
n im3ḫ(w) rḫ-nsw mry nb=f	for the revered one, king's advisor beloved of his lord,
m-r pr s3-ḥwt-ḥr m3ˁ-ḫrw	the steward Sahathor, the justified,
ḥmt=f mrt=f ḫw	(and) his beloved wife Khu.

(the formula is finished off by the inscriptions above the figures of Sahathor and Khu)

Offering-bearers:

s3=f mry=f m-r pr s3-mnḫt m3ˁ-ḫrw	His beloved son, the steward Samenkhet, the justified.
m-r st intf	The overseer of the storehouse Intef.
wb3 m-s3=f	The cup-bearer Emsaf.

Second offering formula:

ḥtp-di-nsw	An offering which the king gives
3sir nb imnt nfrt	to Osiris, lord of the beautiful west,
nṭr ˁ3 nb 3bḏw	great god, lord of Abydos,
di=f mw ḥnḳt snṭr mrḥt	so that he may give water and beer, incense and unguent
ḫt nb(t) nfr(t) wˁb(t)	and everything good and pure
ˁnḫt nṭr im	on which a god lives
m 3bd m ?-nt	at the month-festival, at the half-month festival
w3g ḏḥwtt	the Wag-festival and the Thoth-festival
ḏ3t nṭr r pḳr	and the (festival of) the god's boat-journey to Poker
n im3ḫ(w) m-r pr s3-imn m3ˁ-ḫrw	for the revered one, the steward Saamun, the justified,
ḥmt=f mrt=f ḫw	(and) his beloved wife Khu.

(once again the formula is finished off by the inscriptions above the figures of Saamun and Khu)

Offering-bearers:

wb3 sḥtp-ib	The cup-bearer Sehetepib.
ḫnms=f mry=f intf	His beloved friend Intef.

5.6 *Study Exercise: BM EA 571 (bottom)*

Transliteration and Translation:
a. Family:

s3=f mry=f imny	His beloved son Ameny.
ḥmt=f mrt=f s3t-wsr(t)	His beloved wife Satwosret.
s3=f mry=f ḥm-nṭr s-n-wsrt	His beloved son the priest Senwosret.
ḥmt=f mrt=f s3t-mnṭw	His beloved wife Satmentju.
s3=f mry=f m-r pr imn-m-ḥ3t	His beloved son the steward Amenemhet.
mwt=f bt	His mother Bet.

You may have noticed that the use of 'his' renders the precise reconstruction of genealogies rather problematic. Here the male figures are given in relation to either Sahathor or Saamun (the principal male figures in the offering scenes above), whereas the pairing of male and female figures seems to relate the females to their accompanying male figure rather than directly to either Sahathor or Saamun.

b. Household and estate:

šmsw ṯ3w	The attendant Tjau.	*wb3t ḥtp*	The cup-bearer Hetep.
ḥrt-pr ḫw	The domestic Khu.	*ˁḳ(y)t ddt*	The entering-maid Dedet.
sfṯw s3-ḥwt-ḥr	The butcher Sahathor.	*rḫty s3-ḥwt-ḥr*	The washerman Sahathor.

Chapter 6

6.2 Words:

	ḏr		mi
	nḏ		ḫsf
	mity		sḏrt
	sḳd		šms

6.3 Translation:

a. iw ḳrs.n=i iз(w)   I   buried the old,
        ḥbs.n=i ḥзy   I clothed the naked,
        n ir(=i) iwit r rmṯ   and I did no wrong against people.

b. iw di.n(=i)   t n ḥḳr   I   gave bread   to the hungry
                    ḥbs(w) n ḥзy   and clothes to the naked;
        n srḫ(=i) ˁз(w)   I did not complain about the great,
        sḳbḥ.n(=i) nḏs(w)   and I put the lowly at (their) ease.

c. iw sˁз.n=f w(i)   He   advanced me,
        sḫnt.n=f st(=i)   he promoted my position,
        di.n=f w(i) m st ḥrt-ib=f   and placed me in his confidence
        m ˁḥ=f n wˁˁw   in his private palace (palace of privacy).

6.4 Translation:

iw=i ḥr mˁk ḏr pзt   I have been roasting since the beginning of time -
n mз=i mity srw pn   I have never seen the like of this goose.

6.5 Study exercise: The Osiris Mysteries at Abydos:

a. Transliteration and Translation

1 iw ir.n=i prt wp-wзwt   I   conducted the procession of Wepwawet,
        wḏз=f r nḏ it=f   when he set out to protect his father;
        ḫsf.n=i sbi(w) ḥr nšmt   I drove away the rebels at the Neshmet-bark;
        sḫr.n=i ḫft(w) зsir   and I felled the enemies of Osiris.
   iw ir.n=i prt ˁзt   I   conducted the great procession,
        šms=i nṯr r nmtt=f   following the god at his travels;
        di.n=i sḳd dpt-nṯr   and I made the god's boat sail.

2 iw ḏsr.n=i wз(w)t nṯr   I   cleared the ways of the god
        r mˁḥˁt=f ḫntt pḳr   to his tomb at the forefront of Poker.
   iw nḏ.n=i wnn-nfr   I   protected Wenennefer
        hrw pf n ˁḥз ˁз   on that day of the great fight;
        sḫr.n=i ḫft(w)=f nb   I felled all his enemies
        ḥr ṯsw n ndyt   on the bank of Nedyet
        di.n=i wḏз=f r ḥnw wrt   and I had him proceed inside the great bark.

3 in.n=s зsir ḫnty-imntw   (and) it brought Osiris Khentyimentu
        nb зbḏw n ˁḥ=f   lord of Abydos to his palace,
        šms.n=i nṯr r pr=f   and I followed the god to his house.

6.6 Study exercise: BM EA 586

a. Text:

rnpt-sp 14 ḥr ḥm n nsw-bity	Year 14 under the person of the king of Upper and Lower
ḫpr-kꜣ-rꜥ ꜥnḫ ḏt	Egypt Kheperkare living forever.
imꜣḫ(w) it-nṯr ity ḏd=f	The revered one, the god's father Ity says:
iw wḥm.n(=i) ḥst ḥr nsw	I repeated favour before the king
sꜥꜣ ib(=i) r it(w)(=i)	and advanced my heart more than my forefathers
ḫprw r-ḥꜣt=i	who existed before me.
iw ṯs.n -n=i ḥm=f ḫtm ꜥꜣ	His person assigned to me a great seal
m ḥsmn wꜥb	in pure amethyst,
mi šps-nsw nb	just like any dignitary of the king,
ꜣryt=i m hbny swꜥbt m ḏꜥm	and my staff in ebony decorated in electrum.
imꜣḫ(w) it-nṯr ity	The revered one, the god's father Ity.
ḥmt=f mrt=f iwri	His beloved wife Iuri.

b. The family:

sꜣ=f intf	His son Intef.
sꜣ=f imn-m-ḥꜣt	His son Amenemhet.
sꜣt=f sꜣt-sbk	His daughter Satsobek.
sꜣt=f sꜣt-wsrt	His daughter Satwosret.

Chapter 7

7.2 Words:

	nḏm		*kmꜣ*
	ḫr		*wḏ*
	nḫt		

7.4 Translation:

a.

ink nḏs iḳr	I was an astute individual
ḏd m r=f	who spoke with his (own) mouth,
ir m ḫpš=f	who acted with his (own) strong arm,
sḥsf nwt=f r=f	and who kept his town at a distance from himself.
ink šps m wꜣst	I was a dignitary in Thebes,
iwn ꜥꜣ m ḫntyt	and a great pillar in Khentyt.
iw swꜣ.n(=i) mity(=i) nb	I surpassed any peer of mine
m nwt tn m špss nb	in this town in all kinds of dignity/wealth.

b.

bꜣk=f mꜣꜥ n st-ib=f	His true servant of his affection,
ḫnt(y) st m pr nb=f	one foremost of position in the house of his lord;
sr ꜥꜣ n ib=f	an official great of his heart,
rḫ ḥrt-ib nb=f	one who knows the desire of his lord,
šms sw r nmtt=f nb(t)	one who follows him at all his journeys.

7.5 Stela of Ity (BM EA 586):

imꜣḫ(w) it-nṯr mry nb=f mꜣꜥ	The revered one the god's father, one truly beloved of his lord,
ḥr(y)-sštꜣ n imn-rꜥ m st=f nb	the master of secrets of Amun-Ra in any place of his,
ity ms-n sꜣt-sbk	Ity born of Satsobek.

(honorific transposition of *nb=f* 'his lord')

7.6 *Relative forms:*

ddt pt kmзt tз	which the sky gives, which the land creates,
innt ḥʿp(y)	and which the inundation brings.

7.7 *Study exercise: BM EA 558*

ḥtp-di-nsw	An offering which the king gives
зsir nb ddw ntr ʿз nb зbdw	to Osiris, lord of Djedu, great god, lord of Abydos,
di=f prt-ḥrw	so that he may give a voice offering of
t ḥnkt kз зpd šs mnḫt	bread and beer, ox and fowl, alabaster and linen,
ḫt nb(t) nfr(t) wʿb(t) ʿnḫt ntr im	and everything good and pure on which a god lives
n kз n imзḫ(w) ky	for the ka of the revered one Key,
rḫ-nsw mзʿ mry=f	a true king's adviser beloved of him
ir(r) ḥs(s)t nsw	who does what the king favours
m ḥrt-hrw nt rʿ nb	during the course of every day.
ii(.n=i) m nwt(=i)	I have come from my town;
hз.n(=i) m spзt(=i)	I have descended from my district.
ink dd nfrt	I was one who said what is good,
mrrt ḥrp rḫ-nsw	and what the director of king's advisers loves.
n dws(=i) s n ḥry-tp=f	I did not denounce a man to his superior;
n wd(=i) ḥwt m s=i	I did not command a beating for a man of mine.
imзḫ(w) ḫr ntr ʿз	The revered one before the great god
wḥm ky ms-n mrti mзʿ-ḥrw	the reporter Key, born of Merti, the justified.

7.8 *Study exercise: BM EA 143*

ḥtp-di-nsw	An offering which the king gives
зsir nb ddw ntr ʿз nb зbdw	to Osiris, lord of Djedu, great god, lord of Abydos,
di=f prt-ḥrw	so that he may give a voice offering of
t ḥnkt kз зpd šs mnḫt	bread and beer, ox and fowl, alabaster and linen,
ḫt nbt nfrt wʿbt ʿnḫt ntr im	and everything good and pure on which a god lives,
ddt pt kmзt tз	which the sky gives, which the land creates,
innt ḥʿp(y)	and which the innundation brings
m ḥtp-di-nsw	as an offering which the king gives,
tзw n ʿnḫ ndm st sntr wʿb	the sweet breath of life, and the scent of pure incense
n kз n hзty-ʿ nḫti mзʿ-ḥrw	for the ka of the governor Nakhti, the justified,
ms-n nḫti mзʿt-ḥrw	born of Nakhti, the justified.

Below (from right to left):

ḥmt=f nbt-pr nt-nbw mзʿt-ḥrw	His wife, the mistress of the house Netnebu, the justified.
mwt=f nbt-pr nḫti mзʿt-ḥrw	His mother, the mistress of the house Nakhti, the justified.
mnʿt зst	The wet-nurse Iset.

Chapter 8

8.2 *Words:*

	šsp		*sзḫ*
	mʿḥʿt		*šnyt*
	is		*зḫ*

8.3 BM EA 567:

rnpt-sp 13 ḥr ḥm n	Regnal year 13 under the person of
nsw-bity nbw-k3w-rˁ	the king of Upper and Lower Egypt Nubkaure,
di ˁnḫ ḏt r nḥḥ	given life enduringly and repeatedly.
ḥtp-di-nsw	An offering which the king gives
3sir nb ḏdw ḫnty-imntw nb 3bḏw	to Osiris, lord of Djedu, Khentyimentu, lord of Abydos
wp-w3wt ḫnty 3bḏw	and Wepwawet, the one at the forefront of Abydos,
ḥkt ḥnˁ ḫnmw	Heket and Khnum
nṯrw nb 3bḏw	and all the gods of Abydos
di=sn prt-ḥrw	so that they may give a voice offering of
t ḥnkt k3 3pd šs mnḫt	bread and beer, ox and fowl, alabaster and linen,
ḫt nbt nfr(t) pr(r)t m-b3ḥ nṯr ˁ3	and everything good which goes before the great god.
ms.t(w) n=f ˁwy ḫr ḥtp	May hands be presented to him carrying offerings
m ḥb(w) nw ḫrt-nṯr	during the festivals of the necropolis
ḥnˁ šms(w) n 3sir	along with the followers of Osiris,
tp(w)-ˁ ḫprw ḫr-ḥ3t	the ancestors who existed before.
s3ḫ ṯw wr(w) nw ḏdw	May the great ones of Djedu
šnyt imt 3bḏw	and the entourage in Abydos enspirit you.
ḏd.t(w) n=f iiw m ḥtp	May 'Welcome in peace' be said to him
in wrw nw 3bḏw	by the great ones of Abydos.
sḏ3=f ḥnˁ nṯr ˁ3	May he travel with the great god
m ḏ3t-nṯr r r-pḳr	during the god's journey to Ro-Poker,
nšmt wrt r nmtt=s	when the great Neshmet-bark is at its journeys
m ḥb(w) nw ḫrt-nṯr	during the festivals of the necropolis.
sdm=f hnw m r n t3-wr	May he hear jubilation in the mouth of Tawer
h3kr grḥ n sḏrt	(at) the Haker-rites of the night of vigil
m sḏryt nt ḥr-šn	during the vigil of Horus-*šn*.

8.4 Study exercise: BM EA 584

ḥtp-di-nsw	An offering which the king gives
3sir nb ḏdw ḫnty-imntw	to Osiris, lord of Djedu, Khentyimentu
<nṯr> ˁ3 nb 3bḏw	great (god), lord of Abydos,
wp-w3wt nb t3 ḏsr	Wepwawet, lord of the sacred land,
ḫnmw ḥnˁ ḥkt	Khnum and Heket
nṯrw nbw smyt imntt	and all the gods of the western desert,
di=sn prt-ḥrw	so that they may give a voice offering of
t ḥnkt k3 3pd šs mnḫt	bread and beer, ox and fowl, alabaster and linen,
ḥtp ḏf(3w)	offerings and provisions
n k3 n im3ḫ(w)	for the ka of the revered one
m-r iḳdw ḫw-n-bik ḏd	the overseer of builders Khunenbik, who says:
i ˁnḫw sw3t(y).sn ḥr mˁḥˁt tn	O the living who may pass by this tomb
m ḫd m ḫsft	in going north or in going south,
m mrr=ṯn šms wp-w3wt r nmtt=f nb	in that you wish to follow Wepwawet at all his journeys,
ḏd=ṯn t ḥnkt ḫ3 k3 3pd ḫ3	may you say: 'Bread and beer, 1000, ox and fowl, 1000,
šs mnḫt ḫ3 ḥtp ḏf(3w) ḫ3	alabaster and linen, 1000, offerings and provisions, 1000,
m ḫt nb(t) nfrt wˁbt ˁnḫt nṯr im	as everything good and pure on which a god lives
n k3 n im3ḫy ḫr nṯr(w) nb(w) 3bḏw	for the ka of the revered one before all the gods of Abydos
ḫr nsw	and before the king,

m-r iḳdw ḫw-n-bik mзˁ-ḫrw	the overseer of builders Khuenbik, the justified,
ms-n rrwt	born of Rerut'.

The family:

ḥmt=f ḥwt-ḥr ms-n mзi-n-ḥr	His wife Hathor, born of Mainenhor.
sзt=f rrw(t) mзˁ(t)-ḫrw	His daughter Rerut, the justified.
in sз=f sˁnḫ rn=f	It is his son who has made his name live (on)
m-r iḳdw n-ptḥ-kз(w)	the overseer of builders Niptahkau.
sз=f mry=f ptḥ-ḥtp	His beloved son Ptahhotep.

8.5 *Study exercise: BM EA 162*

ḥtp-di-nsw	An offering which the king gives/places
ḫr зsir ḫnty-imntw	before Osiris-Khentyimentu,
[nṯr ˁз nb] зbḏw	[great god, lord] of Abydos
m s(w)t=f nbt nfrt wˁbt	in all his good and pure places,
di=f prt-ḫrw	so that he may give a voice offering
m t m ḥnḳt	in bread and in beer
m kз зpd m ḫt nb(t) nfrt	in ox and fowl and in everything good
n kз n imзḫw ḫr nṯr ˁз	for the ka of the revered one before the great god,
m-r mšˁ wr imny	the general-in-chief Ameny,
ir-n ḳbw mзˁ-ḫrw	born of Kebu, the justified.
di.t(w) n=f ˁwy m nšmt	May help be given to him in the Neshmet-bark
ḫr wз(w)t imnt	on the ways of the West.
šsp=f ḥtpt ḥr ḥtp ˁз	May he receive offerings (from) upon the great altar
m ḥb(w) n ḫrt-nṯr	during the festivals of the necropolis.
ḏd.t(w) n=f iw m ḥtp	May 'Welcome in peace' be said to him
in wr(w) n зbḏw	by the great ones of Abydos
m wзg m ḏhwtt	at the Wag-festival, at the Thoth-festival,
m ḥb-skr m prt-mnw	at the Soker-festival, at the procession of Min,
m prt spdt m tp-rnpt	at the procession of Sothis, at the begining of the lunar year,
m ḥb(w) nb ˁз irrw	and at all the great festivals which are performed
n зsir ḫnty-imntw nṯr ˁз	for Osiris-Khentyimentu, the great god,
n kз n m-r mšˁ wr imny	for the ka of the general-in-chief Ameny

Family, colleagues and staff in central scene:

ḥmt=f mrt=f	His beloved wife
irrt ḥsst=f rˁ nb	who does what he favours every day
ḥm(t)-nṯr ḥwt-ḥr mdḥw	the priestess of Hathor Medhu,
mst-n imny mзˁt-ḫrw	born of Ameny, the justified.
wbзt sзt-ḫnt-ḫty	The cup-bearer Satkhenetkhety.
bзk=f mзˁ n st-ib=f	His true servant of his affection,
irr ḥsst=f rˁ nb	who does what he favours every day
m-r ḫtmt sз-ḥwt-ḥr	the treasurer Sahathor,
nb imзḫ mзˁ-ḫrw	possessor of reverence, the justfied.
sn=f mr(y)=f ḫnt-ḫty-ḥtp	His beloved brother Khenetkhetyhetep
ir-n sзt-sbk mзˁ-ḫrw	born of Satsobek, the justified.

Lower scene:

sз-ḫnt-ḫty	Sakhenetkhety.
ḥm-kз ḏз-ḥˁp(y)	The ka-priest Djefahapy.
nšt ḫwyt	the hairdresser Khuyet.
ḥr(y)-pr imny	The domestic Ameny.
ḥr(y)-pr зwtyt	The domestic Sautyt.

Bibliography and further reading

The following bibliography is highly selective and aimed at works which will supplement this book and aid you in further reading and study. We have tried to concentrate on books which are still in print and available through major stockists. However, some works of particular relevance for the topics covered in this book will probably only be found in specialist libraries and these are prefixed with *.

Hieroglyphs

On hieroglyphs, two books in particular can be recommended to complement the early part of this book:

W.V. Davies, *Egyptian Hieroglyphs*, Reading the Past series, British Museum Press, London 1987.

J. Malek, *ABC of Egyptian Hieroglyphs*, Ashmolean Museum, Oxford 1994.

Kings' names

A fuller list of the cartouches of the kings of Egypt can be found in:

S.J. Quirke, *Who were the Pharaohs? A History of their Names with a List of their Cartouches*, British Museum Press, London 1990.

Stelae

If you are interested in extending your reading of stelae and coffins, then examples for study are on display in most major museums. In the UK, the following museums have particularly suitable collections (the list is not exhaustive and a number of other museums and private collections also have Middle Kingdom stelae and coffins on display):

Southern England: British Museum, London; Ashmolean Museum, Oxford; Fitzwilliam Museum, Cambridge.

Northern England: Merseyside County Museum, Liverpool; The Manchester Museum; The Oriental Museum, Durham.

Scotland: Royal Museum of Scotland, Edinburgh; Kelvingrove Art Gallery and Museum, Glasgow.

However, if you have access to a good specialist library (such as the library of the Egypt Exploration Society, open to members of the society) then the following two works contain a number of interesting stelae for study:

The most convenient collection of Abydos stelae remains:

> * W.K. Simpson, *The Terrace of the Great God at Abydos: The Offering Chapels of Dynasties 12 and 13.*, Publications of the Pennsylvania–Yale Expedition to Egypt No. 5, Peabody Museum of Natural History and The University Museum of the University of Pennsylvania, New Haven and Philadelphia 1974.

(This book contains photographs of a number of Abydene Middle Kingdom stelae from museum collections around the world, including some of the stelae studied here, reassembled by Simpson into the original groups of monuments found at Abydos.)

The following title contains a number of stelae from Nagʿ ed-Deir of a similar kind to BM EA 1783 (p. 74):

> * D. Dunham, *Naga-ed-Dêr stelae of the First Intermeditate Period*, Museum of Fine Arts, Boston 1937.

Coffins

A convenient introduction to coffins and their development is:

> J.H. Taylor, *Egyptian Coffins*, Shire Publications, Aylesbury 1989.

A more detailed discussion of Middle Kingdom coffins can be found in:

> * H.O. Willems, *Chests of Life: A Study of the Typology and Conceptual Development of Middle Kingdom Standard Class Coffins*, Orientaliste, Leuven 1988.

Religion: Osiris and the afterlife

A convenient recent account is provided in:

> S.J. Quirke, *Ancient Egyptian Religion*, British Museum Press, London 1992 (especially Chapters 2 and 5).

Titles

There is no readily available general work on titles to aid you in your reading. However, a convenient listing of titles by function can be found in:

> * S.J. Quirke, 'The regular titles of the late Middle Kingdom', *Revue d'Égyptologie* 37 (1986), pp. 107-30.

Otherwise, the major listing of Middle Kingdom titles with hieroglyphs, transliteration and translation is:

> * W.A. Ward, *Index of Egyptian Administrative and Religious Titles of the Middle Kingdom, with a Glossary of Words and Phrases Used*, American University in Beirut Press, Beirut 1982.

Translations

The most convenient set of translations for Middle Kingdom stelae (which includes a number of, but far from all, the examples in this book) is:

    * M. Lichtheim, *Ancient Egyptian Autobiographies chiefly of the Middle Kingdom: A Study and an Anthology,* Orbis Biblicus et Orientalis 84, Universitätsverlag, Freiburg and Vandenhoeck & Ruprecht, Göttingen 1988.
Some stelae are also included in Lichtheim's earlier and more readily available book:

    M. Lichtheim, *Ancient Egyptian Literature, I: The Old and Middle Kingdoms,* University of California Press, Berkeley and Los Angeles 1973.
A more recent anthology of translations from a variety of Middle Kingdom texts, including stelae, is:

    R.B. Parkinson, *Voices from Ancient Egypt. An Anthology of Middle Kingdom Writings,* British Museum Press, London 1991.

Dictionaries and sign-lists
The most convenient dictionary in English remains:

    R.O. Faulkner, *A Concise Dictionary of Middle Egyptian,* Griffith Institute, Oxford 1962.
A more comprehensive sign-list with an extensive discussion of the use of signs is included at the end of:

    A.H. Gardiner, *Egyptian Grammar, Being an Introduction to the Study of Hieroglyphs.* 3rd edition, Griffith Institute, Oxford 1957.
Both of these works are still in print and readily available.

Grammar
Gardiner's *Egyptian Grammar* also remains the most comprehensive treatment of ancient Egyptian in English, although a number of the sections on the verb (occupying the second half of the book) are now rather dated.

Our book is not intended as a grammar book, but lying behind the presentation of the language is the particular 'verbalist' approach developed by Mark Collier in a number of specialist papers. A similar 'verbalist' approach is conveniently presented in:

    A. Loprieno, *Ancient Egyptian: A Linguistic Introduction,* Cambridge University Press, Cambridge 1995.
This book also provides a concise account of the historical development of ancient Egyptian language and scripts.

The authors of this book can be contacted via School for Scribes, PO Box 25020, Glasgow G1 5YD, United Kingdom.

Index

abbreviations, *see* words

Abydos 41, 54–6, 58, 73, 87–9, 121, 124; Abydos formula 114–15; *see also* Osiris

adjectives 10, 93–4, 117–18, 150; as nouns 94, 150; genitival adjective 40

agreement 10, 19, 71, 93–4, 96, 100–101, 111, 116, 117, 148, 150

Anubis 42, 63–4

appeal to the living 111–14

auxiliaries 66–7, 80–81, 82, 83–4

captions 49–50

causation 82, 115

characterisation 68–9, 96–8

cartouches 20, 26, 28

coffins 62–4

compound expressions 40

continuation 80–81, 82

co-ordination, without linking words 67, 80–81, 84–5

dating 21

dating criteria 38, 39, 41, 107, 110, 114

defective writings, *see* words

description 65, 68, 80

determinatives (meaning-signs) 5–6, 13

direction of writing, *see* words

Djedu 41

duals, dual endings 19, 149

dynasties (of kings) 22

epithets, *see* titles

ethical behaviour 35, 65, 75

family, *see* kinship

feminine, *see* nouns, gender; *see also* agreement

festivals 50, 76–8, 123; *see also* Osiris

filiation, *see* kinship

First Intermediate Period 22

funerary beliefs 35, 50, 76–8, 87, 114–15

funerary cult *see* offerings

future, *see* tenses

genitive (possessor) 39–40, 98–9, 150; *see also* adjectives

graphic transposition, *see* word order

Haker-rites 87–9

honorific transposition, *see* word order

Horus: name of king 20; son of Osiris 41–2, 71, 121; four sons of 62–3

ideograms (sound-meaning signs) 17–18

infinitive 49–50, 52–4, 144–5

Inhuret 70, 73

Isis 41–2

Khentyimentu, *see* Osiris

Index of illustrations (monuments from the British Museum collection)